JEWS & CHRISTIANS

A Troubled Family

Walter Harrelson
&
Randall M. Falk

Abingdon Press
Nashville

JEWS AND CHRISTIANS: A TROUBLED FAMILY

Copyright © 1990 by Abingdon Press

96 97 98 99 00 01 02—10 9 8

This book is printed on recycled, acid-free paper.

Library of Congress Cataloging-in-Publication Data

HARRELSON, WALTER.
 Jews & Christians : a troubled family / Walter Harrelson & Randall M. Falk.
 p. cm.
 Includes bibliographical references and index.
 ISBN 0-687-20332-5 (alk. paper)
 1. Judaism—Relations—Christianity. 2. Christianity and other religions—
Judaism. I. Falk, Randall M. II. Title.
 BM535.H32   1990
 261.2'6—dc20   90-35783

Scripture quotations noted JPS are from *The Torah*, copyright © 1962, and *The Prophets* copyright © 1978 by the Jewish Publication Society of America.

Scripture quotations noted RSV are from the Revised Standard Version of the Bible, copyright 1946, 1952, 1971 by the Division of Christian Education of the National Council of Churches of Christ in the USA. Used by permission.

Excerpts from *A Christian Theology of the People Israel* by Paul Van Buren. Copyright © 1983 by Paul Van Buren. Reprinted by permission of Harper & Row, Publishers, Inc.

MANUFACTURED IN THE UNITED STATES OF AMERICA

To
Edna and Idella
for every good reason

JEWS & CHRISTIANS

A Troubled Family

CONTENTS

INTRODUCTION

This book began in a classroom of the Divinity School of Vanderbilt University in the spring semester, 1986. We, Professor Walter Harrelson and Rabbi Randall Falk, long-time friends and associates in varied campus and communal activities, felt there was a real need for a graduate seminar that emphasized the historical and theological foundations for positive Jewish-Christian relationships. We therefore decided to offer a seminar on Judaism and Christianity: Historical Perspectives and Contemporary Concerns.

The response, both in terms of the number of students enrolled from the Divinity School and the Graduate Department of Religion and in terms of the students' depth of interest in the subject matter, was so encouraging that we agreed to teach the course together again the following year. The Divinity School's Department of Continuing Education also requested that we condense the seminar into six sessions and present it at a local church for the entire community. The enrollment for such evening courses was usually twenty-five to thirty persons. We were overwhelmed with an enrollment of one hundred and sixty-seven for this seminar, the vast majority of whom maintained regular attendance throughout the six weeks.

Because of this manifest interest in the subject, we were invited to present three of the seminars for a Vanderbilt alumni group in Birmingham, Alabama, and a similar series at another Nashville church in the spring of 1989. For the academic year 1989–90 we accepted invitations to lead these seminars on Jewish-Christian relations in Montreal, Memphis, and Huntsville.

We have often asked ourselves: how can we account for the

9

large numbers of adult men and women in all age categories who enroll in these seminars? We have concluded that there are two most significant answers.

In the first place, both Christians and Jews recognize how very little we know about each other's beliefs and practices, historical backgrounds, and particular concerns about the present situations and the future aspirations of our constituencies. We come together in businesses and professions. We meet frequently in civic organizations and for philanthropic undertakings. In recent years, we have begun to see social barriers between Christians and Jews crumble. And yet, we still know so little about each other's religions. Except for some life-cycle occasions, we rarely visit each other's houses of worship. Like politics, religion is usually considered a taboo subject on social occasions. What little we do know about each other's traditions is often tainted by inherited prejudices in families, in church or synagogue teaching, and in discriminatory clubs and organizations.

Fortunately, in a more open, free society, many of the old prejudices are being questioned and examined. Consequently men and women are beginning to seek factual information about the religions of their neighbors. The more we question and refute inherited tales and myths, the more we realize that Judaism and Christianity stand together on common ground in much of our heritage and in many of our teachings.

Despite the fact that we have come to realize that the moral truths and ethical principles taught by our two faiths are virtually identical, and despite the understanding that our values and our goals so closely parallel each other's, we also recognize that there are theological beliefs and social issues in which we often have profound differences. Just as it is important that we recognize how much we share in common, it is equally important that we understand and respect each other's freedom to differ. It is rarely a matter of who is right and who is wrong. Nor is it possible to determine objectively whether a better answer is offered by one group or the other to a common problem or concern.

The more we study and the more we share our quests for truth, the more we recognize that there are many paths that lead up the mountain toward the same pinnacle. It is not essential, or even desirable, that we walk the same path. It is important, however,

10

that we understand the beliefs that direct our respective journeys, the hazards we face along the way, and the ultimate aspiration of both Jews and Christians: to fulfill our covenants with the One God as God's partners in seeking salvation here and hereafter.

The goal of our seminars and of this book, then, is to provide basic knowledge in the most crucial areas of Jewish and Christian traditions and beliefs, and to present enough background information to make these understandable. Then our hope is that we can pose the right questions for you to be able to pursue your continuing search for more profound appreciation both of your own heritage and that of your neighbor. When we acquire greater insight into the wisdom of both Jewish and Christian legacies, and when, on this foundation of knowledge, we build a mutual respect for our own heritage and that of our neighbor, we can together aspire to fulfill our covenant with the one God: to be co-workers with God in seeking salvation for ourselves and for all humankind in a just and compassionate society in this world, and in eternal peace hereafter.

CHAPTER ONE

HOW WE VIEW EACH OTHER

A Jewish Outlook

And some of my best friends are Christians?!" is the sardonic response of many Jews who are more than slightly cynical when confronted with the well meant, but condescendingly perceived: "Some of my best friends are Jews." Though Jewish-Christian relationships have come a long way since the medieval European ghetto walls crumbled, interpersonal relationships beyond the marketplace are only beginning to penetrate the five o'clock curtain that upper-middle-class WASPS have regularly lowered to maintain separation, not of church and state, but of social intercourse between Christians and Jews.

The winds of change are blowing, though, across college campuses and through the pristine halls of country clubs. Fraternity/sorority barriers to minorities are slowly disappearing; city clubs and some country clubs, through necessity or by choice, have cracked their doors. Civic organizations and community programs have made even greater strides in the integration process. Business, professional, and higher educational opportunities are open to all minorities on a grander scale than ever before; only large industry's and utility's executive suites remain mostly closed to minority representation. The American Dream is closer to fulfillment for racial, ethnic, and religious minorities.

Much credit for this changing environment must be given to the Roman Catholic Church, since Vatican Council II, and to the mainline Protestant churches. The elimination of old prejudicial stereotypes is only one facet of the challenge the churches have confronted. Even more important has been the teaching in the pulpits and Sunday school classrooms that Christianity's foundations rest on sturdy Jewish pillars of Scripture, history, and sacred covenantal bonds.

In 1975, the National Conference of Catholic Bishops issued this statement:

> Most essential concepts in the Christian creed grew at first in Judaic soil. Uprooted from that soil, these basic concepts cannot be perfectly understood. It is for reasons such as these that the Second Vatican Council in *Nostra aetate* recommends joint "theological and biblical studies" with Jewish scholars. The renewal of Christian faith is the issue here, for renewal always entails to some extent a return to one's origins.

A recent statement from the Presbyterian Church echoes this sentiment:

> Christianity began in the context of Jewish life and faith. Jesus was a Jew as were his earliest followers. . . . The life and liturgy of the Jews provided the language and thought forms through which the revelation in Jesus was first received and expressed.

The Christian and Jewish academic and theological communities work together more harmoniously than ever before. Churches and synagogues across America have become increasingly close through joint study and sharing of vital social justice concerns. The revision of liturgical materials and the editing of Sunday school texts to eliminate anti-Semitic references have had a salutary effect. Equally important has been the church-synagogue leadership for the private sector in seeking to fill the void left by governmental curtailment of programs for the hungry, the homeless, and the sick.

And yet, with all the progress that has been made, old stereotypes remain to haunt and harry us. Despite the earnest efforts of Christian clergy and informed laity, many fundamentalist Christians still see Jews as unrepentant Christ-killers, as a stubborn, stiff-necked remnant who reject Jesus as their Lord and Savior. They believe that Jews have successfully impeded the Second Coming and have resisted the missionary zeal of those intent upon making the United States a Christian nation. These same Christians have perpetuated the literary stereotypes of Jews as crass moneylenders, grasping merchants whose business tactics condone cheating and taking advantage of the helpless gentile.

These stereotypes have been greatly exacerbated in the Black community of America, where most serious racial/religious prejudices confront the Jewish community. Some of this stereotyping occurs because there has been so little opportunity for the two communities to meet on common ground. Some comes because Blacks see Jews as those who take advantage of them in credit stores, in housing rentals, or as domestic servants. Some of the prejudices must be laid at the feet of uneducated Black clergypersons who perpetuate the prejudices handed down through the generations. Much of the often bitter relationship between Blacks and Jews also results from the perception that the State of Israel, and thus all Jews, are enemies and oppressors of the Third World, the "disadvantaged" and "downtrodden" Arabs with whom many American Blacks identify, despite the historic fact that it was the Arabs who originally sold the Blacks into slavery.

Jews also are burdened with inherited and acquired stereotypes that become barriers in relationships with Christians. Past generations bequeath the image of Christians who seek to make of the Jews second-class citizens with limited economic and educational opportunities and with many political and civil disabilities. Jews also see Christians, on the one hand, as excluding them from their social clubs and festivities, and, on the other hand, as seeking to convert Jews and bring them into the church.

In more recent times Jews have seen Christians as the passive observers while six million Jews perished in the Holocaust. Christians also are perceived as having allowed the State of Israel to stand alone, except for the help of diaspora Jewry, as the Arab world tried, through three wars, to complete Hitler's genocide against Jews, by attacking the young State created by the United Nations.

These, then, are the stereotypes often held by White and Black Christians, and by Jews, which perpetuate old prejudices and create new tensions between our groups. Part of the problem is that it is difficult for Jews to erase from their minds and hearts more than two thousand years of bitterness and misunderstanding. While Jews struggled to remain alive as Jews, many Christians struggled with equal tenacity to convert them to acceptance of Jesus as their Messiah, and of the church as providing the path to their salvation. Jews find it difficult to unlearn the lessons that history has taught so painfully. Christians are equally limited in their outreach by a literal reading of the New Testament and by their own concept of mission to the Jews.

Nevertheless, progress has been made in improving Christian-Jewish understanding and relationships in the last half of the twentieth century. The beginning of dialogue, on many different levels, has at least opened the doors for further study and for person-to-person contact. In our churches and synagogues, in our homes and our clubs, we are beginning to talk and to trust. Once we know each other better, we find there are many things we can do together, especially in the areas of social welfare and of mutual concern for the survival of our environment and of the human race. The late Abraham Heschel put it best when he said:

> Religion becomes sinful when it begins to advocate the segregation of God, to forget that the true sanctuary has no walls. Religion has always suffered from the tendency to become an end in itself, to seclude the holy, to become parochial, self-indulgent, self-seeking; as if the task were not to ennoble human nature but to enhance the power and beauty of its institutions or to enlarge the body of doctrines. It has often done more to canonize prejudices than to wrestle for truth; to petrify the sacred than to sanctify the secular. Yet the task of religion is to be a challenge to the stabilization of values. (From *God in Search of Man* [Northvale, N.J.: Jason Aronson, 1987], p. 414)

We are beginning to see that Jews and Christians are not each other's mortal enemies. All of us are confronted by the callousness of secularism. We share the tragedies of war and poverty, of loss of freedom at the hand of tyrants, and of loss of moral imperatives in the scientists' race to perfect weapons of destruction and to develop formulas for control of life, from birth to death. The ethical principles by which we make choices as to how our scientific prowess can best be used for the enhancement and enrichment of life must be formulated by Jews and Christians together for civilization's survival. Unless we develop the kind of mutual respect and cooperation that makes us partners in accepting the challenges that confront us, we shall fail to lead humanity in making the choices that preserve and enrich life. The late Rabbi Morris Adler saw the task ahead so clearly and so compassionately when he said:

> If I were a Christian, I would try to help the Jew to be as Jewish as I the Christian would wish to be Christian. I would say to the Jew: Be Jewish, gloriously, positively, affirmatively, wholesomely Jewish. For this society we must together build, lest paganism and brutality drive out all decency, and God become the greatest refugee of all. We want of you, the Jew, not alone your brawn and the sweat of your brow, but also the distilled wisdom of the centuries, the precious insights of your history, and accumulated riches of your experience, the understanding and tenderness born of your suffering. Give your whole self, as I would give my whole self, so that on the firm Gibraltar of brotherhood we may together build the good life, the city of God, the Kingdom of Heaven.

Conversely, as a Jew, I would try to help the Christian to be as Christian as I the Jew wish to be a Jew. I would say to the Christian: Glory in the teachings of Jesus. Pray his prayer daily, follow in his footsteps to feed the hungry, clothe the naked, and extend a helping hand to all who have lost their way in the world. Strengthen the church, that its clarion call to salvation may be heard in the marketplace and in the high places of government and commerce. Challenge bigotry and oppression, greed and lust for power, through your missions on every continent. Lead the way for men and women of every race and nation and creed to discover the glorious heritage we share and to build on its sturdy foundations a civilization committed to freedom and to peace.

Having recognized a common heritage, and having accepted common goals, we Jews and Christians must determine how we can respectfully deal with the key areas in which we differ. There are some basic issues that Judaism and Christianity approach from quite different historical and theological perspectives. We do not need to compromise in our interpretations of these differences, but we must surely understand them. Rosemary

Ruether, in *Faith and Fratricide,* defines these key issues as the schism of judgment and promise, the schism of particularism and universalism, and the schism of letter and spirit. The overriding issue, however, is Christology. In the chapters that follow we shall examine these issues carefully and in depth, so that the common ground we share may also bear fruit through our appreciation of the uniqueness to be found in each tradition. Ruether also calls on us to recognize that "prophetic religion is a religion of self-criticism." It is urgent in our day, too, that Jews and Christians not only reinforce our respective covenants with God, but that we dedicate ourselves to learning from our failure, that we may serve the one God by sharing fully and wholeheartedly God's Word and bounty with all humankind.

HOW WE VIEW EACH OTHER

A Christian Outlook

C hristian history is deeply disfigured by prejudice against Judaism and mistreatment of the Jewish people. Some features of that story will be reviewed below. Christian history is also marred by longstanding misrepresentation of Judaism within the churches. The result is that Christian worship, teaching, and public witness often have been harmful to good relations between Jews and Christians, even on the part of the most well-meaning of Christians. The situation is so serious that merely to continue Christian education, worship, and witness is to run the risk of continuing Christian prejudice against Judaism and the Jewish people.

Why should that be so? How indeed is it possible that Christians who are taught not to show prejudice against any person or group should pass along prejudice against Jews just by continuing their Christian witness? The answer seems to lie in the way in which Christians pass along the biblical heritage and interpret it.

The "Old" Testament

Consider what it means to use the standard terminology that has existed in the church through the centuries: the Bible consists of two parts, the Old Testament and the New Testament. Surely, no one intended by such terminology to denigrate the Jewish people or show the superiority of Christianity to Judaism. Even so, how easy it has been for this terminology to work to the favor of Christianity and the disfavor of Judaism. The new is surely better than the old; does the old have any value or validity at all? A number of Christian bodies have made the New Testament *the* authority for faith and practice and have, at least implicitly, treated the Hebrew Scriptures as superseded by the New Testament. Over and again, throughout Christian history, the church has been tempted to go the path of the Christian heretic Marcion (flourished 144 c.e.), who rejected the authority of the Hebrew Scriptures entirely, contrasting the cruel deity of the Old Testament with the entirely distinct and loving God of the New Testament.

Sinful Israel

The Hebrew Scriptures testify amply to the faithlessness of God's people. From earliest times, Christians have read these stories of Israel's failures as a basis for the claim that God has rejected Israel in favor of the Christian community. Such a misreading of the Hebrew Scriptures is perhaps understandable on the part of unreflective readers of the Bible. But it is a sad commentary on Christian theological thought that so often this flat and erroneous reading of the Scriptures is found among learned and sophisticated students of the Bible as well.

It is one of the great testimonies to the candor and fearlessness of the biblical writers that they did not hesitate to denounce Israel's sin just as strongly as they denounced the sins of the foreign nations. In fact, Israel's failures to maintain the covenant between God and the people were even more fiercely condemned than were the sins of the surrounding peoples (see Amos 1:3–3:8). But the prophets were not saying that the Israelites were the worst people of the ancient Near Eastern world. Rather, they were insisting that God was depending upon the people of God in very special ways—to see to it that God's teaching reached the ends of the earth, that Israel was a witness in the world, publicly and clearly, to God's way and to God's purposes for all the peoples of earth (see Genesis 12:1-3). Israel's failures, therefore, were no ordinary ones; if the world was to know God's teaching, God's intentions for the creation, Israel had to be a faithful witness to God before all the nations. For this reason, when Israel failed God, the very intentions of God for all the creation were in jeopardy.

On the basis of comparisons with the law codes and teachings and customs of ancient Near Eastern peoples, one is able to say with confidence that ancient Israel was among the most moral and just of ancient peoples. It makes no sense, therefore, for Christians or others to take the *theological* denunciations of the prophets as literal truth. The people attacked by the prophets were attacked for their failures to live up to God's *covenant demands*. Of course the people of Israel failed that test, as the Christian community has regularly failed the test of *covenant faithfulness*. But subtly, and without deliberate intent, Christians have turned the grand religious/theological demands of Israel's prophets into flat judgments against the people as a whole.

The next step taken is obvious. Since Israel failed God so gravely, God had no choice but to reject this faithless people and raise up a new people who would not be so faithless—the Christian community! This way of viewing the relations of Jews and Christians appears already in the New Testament, though it is powerfully countered by Paul's insistence that God has by no means rejected the people Israel (Romans 11:1). But in the work of Christian education, how easy it has proved to be to offer an almost classic picture of Israel's history. It goes this way.

When God called Abraham from Ur of the Chaldeans and led him into the land of the promise, Abraham obeyed without question. He and Isaac were faithful to the covenant, and all went well with them. But Jacob proved to be treacherous and a schemer. He managed to secure the birthright from his older brother Esau, and then he tricked his father into giving him the blessing that was intended also for Esau. Moses was a great and faithful leader, but the people he led from slavery to freedom turned on him, proved to be unreliable and faithless, and had to die in the wilderness, outside the promised land. Even Moses, because of his occasional lapses, had to die outside the land of promise.

On entering the good land, granted them by God and delivered into their hands by God, the people took possession, but they were soon drawn away from God and began to worship the gods of the foreign nations. Though often called back to faith in God, they kept sinning and falling away from the true path. God sent foes to punish them and bring them to their senses. But though God did save them over and again when they cried out for help, the people persisted in their sinful ways.

Facing the great threat of the Philistines, they demanded a king to lead them in battle. Samuel, their faithful leader, was told by God to give them a king, and he did so. But neither the kings appointed to lead them nor the people themselves proved to be faithful. Over and again, God brought punishment upon them—famine and drought, blight and mildew, invasion by insects and by hordes of hostile armies—but they would not return and be faithful to God (see Amos 4). Finally, God handed the northern tribes over to the Assyrians (722/721 B.C.E.) and the remaining tribe of Judah over to the Babylonians (587/586 B.C.E.).

Even then, God did not finally give up on Israel, but gave the people one more chance. They were freed by Cyrus of Persia to return from Babylonian exile in 538 B.C.E., and some made their way back. But it was a time of small things. The rebuilt Temple was not worthy of comparison with Solomon's beautiful structure, nor was this small province of Persia comparable with the vast extent of the kingdom of David. The people who had returned from exile remained unable or unwilling to maintain the covenant made by God with them, and, as the Old Testament closes, the prophet Malachi is promising a day to come when God will raise up an Elijah who will call the people to faithfulness and unite the hearts of parents and children in true devotion to God and to one another.

The point is that Christian children have been taught this story of Israelite history and religion through the centuries. But they have not been taught the story as *Israel's own* story of how their ancestors failed God by not holding fast to the divine law and covenant. They have heard the story as though it were a factual account of how sinful and ungrateful the Jews were, so sinful in fact that God had finally to reject them in favor of the Christian community. Such a misreading of the biblical story leaves Christians able to hear the message of Israel's prophets not as a message against *them too*. They can hear Amos and Isaiah and Jeremiah as voices from the past against the Jewish people, not against the covenant people of the Bible, Jews and Christians alike.

The Return from Babylonian Exile

In a similar way, Christians often have viewed the late period in biblical history as a time of decline and loss of religious substance. There *was* some decline in culture and religion during the period following the destruction of Jerusalem in 587/586 B.C.E. and during the long years of restoration after the Jewish exiles began to return from Babylonia after 538 B.C.E. But the decline was not a collapse of religious faith, nor was it a time when prophecy had died or been repudiated. The period was marked by successes and failures, by gains and losses, religiously and culturally. Christians have interpreted this time following the return from exile and up to the birth of Christianity as a time when Judaism was displaying its bankruptcy. That is untruthful and unfair. Judaism was too much under the domination of the priests in Jerusalem during part of this period, and the priesthood did suffer corruption during the period. But Jewish movements, lay movements, against a corrupt priesthood developed during this time. The result was the appearance of the Pharisees and the institution of the synagogue. Another result was the development of a hope in God's restoration of Israel's life and faith under new leadership, and this hope was to a large extent realized in two ways—in Christianity and in rabbinic Judaism.

Therefore, it is wrong and seriously misleading for the Christian community to see in the post-exilic period a time of material and spiritual decline that demonstrated the need for Judaism to be replaced by Christianity. Judaism in the period just before the birth of Christianity was a complex and religiously vibrant reality. How vibrant it was will be shown when we examine the various Jewish groups and movements at the time of Jesus (see below, chapters 2 and 5).

The Pharisees

One further misunderstanding that has prepared Christians to misjudge Judaism and mistreat Jews is the picture of the scribes and the Pharisees in the New Testament. We shall be speaking more about the Pharisees later on. Here we only want to call attention to the danger of misrepresenting Judaism that emerges in the New Testament's portrayals of the Pharisees. The Judaism

23

that came to dominate the scene through the work of the great rabbinical schools was the Judaism of the Pharisees. The Pharisees were a lay movement against the domination of religion by the priests in Jerusalem. It was the Pharisees who set out to make Torah, God's Law, applicable to all aspects of daily life, relevant to the full range of human needs, and a guide that would make it possible for the ordinary individual and family to serve God faithfully. The Pharisees were not bent on laying a burden on the people; on the contrary, they were determined to make God's teaching applicable to the whole range of human activity.

In the New Testament, we read of conflicts between Jesus and the scribes and Pharisees, conflicts that are very much like those between one rabbinical school of thought and another. Jesus is opposing a narrow interpretation of God's Torah, while his opponents are defending that narrow interpretation. In some respects, of course, Jesus' interpretations too were quite narrow (Matthew 5–7), but in others they were liberal indeed. In any event, the Pharisees were the reformers of their day, calling the people to a faithful life, opposing priestly religion that was corrupt, and insisting that God's will could and must be done in daily life.

Christians ought therefore to be very careful in speaking of the Pharisees as religious bigots or fanatics. They were not that at all, or most of them were not. The problem has been that Christians have tended to judge the Judaism of Jesus' day as though all of it was narrow and bigoted, concerned with only the external aspects of religion, while Christianity was concerned about the heart and soul of religion.

Law and Grace

One further way in which Christians have misjudged Judaism and have strained relations between the two communities also appears in the New Testament. Paul's sharp contrast between law and grace has led to grave misunderstandings. Paul was talking about a form of religious demand that was harsh and unyielding and enslaving of the human spirit. The Torah, or Law, of Judaism was never intended to be such a form of religion. That is clear from the many places in which the Torah was understood in

Israel as a gift of divine love and grace (see especially Psalms 1, 19, and 119). God's Torah was a gift of love, given to Israel to enable the people to know God's demands and to walk in God's ways. To live by Torah was to live by divine love.

But of course people can take a good gift of God and spoil it, making it not a means to freedom but an instrument of enslavement. Paul's attacks on the law (Greek *nomos*) were attacks on *legalism*—on an attitude that can develop in any religion; it has developed from time to time in Judaism, and it certainly has often flourished in Christianity as well. Many interpreters of the New Testament are convinced that when Paul spoke of the law he was often speaking, not of the Jewish Torah, but of legalisms among the non-Jews as well as among the Jews.

Jesus

Finally, the very figure of Jesus has sometimes led the Christian community to be suspicious of Judaism or actually to hate the Jewish people. Jesus comes into the ancient world as the fulfillment of the hopes and longings of the human heart, but especially of the Jewish heart. Jesus' earliest followers were all Jews, just as Jesus was. Jesus is portrayed in the New Testament with such attractiveness and compelling power as to cause those who accept Jesus as their Savior and Friend to wonder why others would not do the same. Especially troubling for many Christians has been the fact that a majority of the Jewish people in Jesus' lifetime did not accept him. Jesus goes to his death on the cross, according to the New Testament, with some Jews assenting to his death and others indeed urging the Roman authorities to crucify him.

Through the centuries, some Christians have continued to consider this fact the chief point of contention with the Jewish people. Note that the New Testament is clear that it was the Roman authorities who put Jesus to death. But Christians continue to be puzzled by the question of what Jews have against Jesus that would have led them (and would lead them today) to reject Jesus as the Promised One. We shall have much more to say about this issue later (especially in chapter 5), but for now it is only necessary to see how the cardinal point in Christian faith, allegiance to Jesus as the Christ, also of course continues to be a point of contention between Jews and Christians.

Summing Up

We can see, therefore, that the very practice of Christianity over the centuries has helped to keep alive the damaging picture of Judaism sketched above. Christians have not, of course, set out to teach their children to hate Judaism and the Jewish people. But the Christian community has inadvertently kept fertile the soil within which Christian mistrust of Judaism has continued to grow.

It is deeply gratifying to see, however, that all of the above points are being regularly challenged within the Christian community today. Church school literature in Catholic and Protestant circles very carefully points out the difference between saying that the Jewish people in biblical times failed God and violated the covenant and saying that ancient Israel was a particularly immoral and corrupt people. Israel was finding it difficult to live up to God's demands, just as people since then have found it hard to do so. Christians find it hard to do so too.

Some churches still present Christianity as the successor religion to Judaism, portraying Judaism as a failure through and through. But a good number of statements adopted by churches in the United States, and by other church bodies worldwide, explicitly repudiate such a view and call for the recognition of the validity of the Jewish witness alongside that of the Christian witness; warn against misunderstandings of the Hebrew Scriptures; point to the scandal of Christian persecution and mistreatment of Jews through the centuries and repent of it, asking for God's forgiveness; and call for continuing dialogue and exchanges between Jewish and Christian bodies so that what remains of prejudice and misunderstanding between the two bodies can in time be eliminated.

This book has arisen to contribute to that end. Today, Christians are learning that Judaism is a partner in religious faith without which the Christian community cannot fulfill its own mission. Judaism may be able to manage without its junior partner Christianity; that is a question for Judaism. But

Christianity cannot fulfill its vocation apart from Judaism, for the Christian witness depends upon the vitality and validity of the Hebrew Scriptures. The Hebrew Scriptures need the interpretative voice of the church, Christians believe, but Christians should also see that the Hebrew Scriptures need the interpretative voice of Israel's oral tradition—Talmud and Midrash—and the continuing reclaiming of the Scriptures by each succeeding generation. No longer, then, can Jews and Christians just go their own way, leaving the other to go its way as it sees fit. At least from the Christian side, conversation and debate and mutual assistance in the search for understanding and public witness are absolutely essential. The Christian witness has much to gain from such joint effort. It is incumbent on Christians to prove worthy of being true and authentic partners in dialogue.

Suggested Readings

(Complete publication information is given in the Bibliography, pages 199-201.)

Croner, H. *Stepping Stones to Further Jewish-Christian Relations.*
Eckardt, A. R. *Elder and Younger Brothers.*
Jacobs, W. *Christianity Through Jewish Eyes.*
Klenicki, L., and G. Wigoder. *A Dictionary of the Jewish-Christian Dialogue.*
Oesterreicher, J. *Brothers in Hope.*
Rousseau, R. W. *Christianity and Judaism: The Deepening Dialogue.*
Ruether, R. *Faith and Fratricide.*
Sandmel, S. *When a Jew and Christian Marry.*
Simon, M. *Verus Israel.*
Tcherikover, V. *Hellenistic Civilization and the Jews.*
Thoma, C. *A Christian Theology of Judaism.*

CHAPTER TWO

HISTORICAL PERSPECTIVES ON THE RELATIONSHIPS OF JEWS AND NON-JEWS

A Jewish Outlook

M any fibers of mind and heart are interwoven to form the warp and woof of Jewish history. It is our purpose, not to illuminate all of these strands, but rather to focus on those which help us better understand the relationship of Jews to our God and to our neighbors. We shall seek especially to comprehend the emerging patterns of Jewish-Christian relationships and the conflicts that disrupted those relationships because of political and economic pressures and theological differences. It is important to understand the rivalries that developed because of competition for proselytes and because of the jousting for power as Jews, Christians, and Muslims all sought to control Palestine, holy to all three, and to dominate the religious life of the Western world. In the latter half of the twentieth century we shall also see a rapprochement between Jews and Christians, as we began to recognize those common roots and similarities of values which unite us against the mounting pressures of secularism.

* * *

The foundation of Judaism is Torah (the five books of Moses). Orthodox Jews believe that Torah was given to the Hebrew people by God through Moses at Sinai. They think of Torah as the revealed Law which cannot be altered in any way. Most Conservative and Reform Jews believe that Torah was not

God-given but rather was God-inspired. Basically we follow the Wellhausen theory that Torah was written by at least four schools, usually referred to as J, E, P, and D (see pages 55-56). The authors of Torah wrote between 850 and 450 B.C.E., and it is generally thought that the five books were brought together in a single scroll around 440 B.C.E. when Ezra, the scribe, wrote that Torah was read in the second Temple on Monday, Thursday, and Saturday mornings. All branches of Judaism agree, however, that no matter whether we consider Torah to be God-given or God-inspired, its teachings are the essence of the covenantal relationship between God and the Jewish people.

Liberal Jewish interpreters of Torah, recognizing that Judaism did not develop in isolation from other cultures, see a synthesis of Torah teachings with those of the religions of other nations. The creation story found in chapters 1 and 2 of the book of Genesis in Hebrew Scriptures can also be found, in large measure, in the folklore of the Egyptians and Babylonians. The authors of Hebrew Scriptures added two unique ethical concepts to the earlier creation stories: the idea that at each step of creation God saw what had been made, and it was good; and the conclusion that God rested on the seventh day, thus establishing that day as the Sabbath. In similar fashion, the Flood narrative in Genesis, chapters 6 through 9, can be traced to earlier folklore. The version in Hebrew Scriptures, however, adds the seven Noahide ethical laws and the concept of a covenant relationship between God and humankind, symbolized by the rainbow.

The most significant instance of synthesis in all of Torah, however, is found in the book of Exodus, chapter 32. Here the Hebrews, restless because of Moses' long absence on the mountain, prevail upon Aaron to make for them a golden calf, that they might worship the god of a neighboring tribe. When Moses returns with the two tablets of laws, there is conflict between those who would be loyal to Yahweh alone, and those who would both heed Yahweh's commandments and worship a neighbor's god, whose image they had replicated for themselves.

This basic conflict between those Jews who would maintain a way of life completely separated from the beliefs and practices of other peoples, and those Jews who would synthesize Jewish teachings with selected aspects of other religions, has existed from biblical times to the present day. It raises the additional question of whether it is better for Jews to live apart from our neighbors, or whether Jews find greater fulfillment of their mission by mingling with the peoples among whom we have lived throughout our history. The ways in which we handle these dilemmas have great bearing on Jewish-Christian relationships today, even as they had profound impact on our relationships with other peoples and their religions in every land in which we have lived.

The Hebrew prophets wrestled with this problem of separatism versus syncretism, and later with the dilemma of particularism versus universalism. On the one hand, the prophets were deeply concerned that the Hebrews worship Yahweh alone. They condemned the desire of some of the people to incorporate, alongside their worship of Yahweh, the worship of deities already established by other peoples in the promised land the Hebrews now occupied. The prophets maintained that the Hebrew people fulfilled their covenant with the one God only if they served Yahweh alone and if they lived by the moral law proclaimed at Sinai. Despite this emphasis on the uniqueness of the covenantal relationship between Yahweh and the Hebrew people, even the earliest literary prophets, Hosea, Amos, Micah, and First Isaiah, began to teach that Yahweh was indeed the God of all peoples, and that the Hebrews should welcome all who chose to accept Yahweh as their God. This concept grew during the period of Babylonian exile, so that Second Isaiah could proclaim: "My House shall be called a house of prayer for all peoples" (Isaiah 56:7 JPS), and in the post-exilic period the prophet Malachi could deliver the climactic challenge of universalism: "Have we not all one father? Did not one God create us? Why do we break faith with one another, profaning the covenant of our fathers?" (Malachi 2:10 JPS).

It was in the post-exilic period, however, that one of the sharpest clashes between particularists and universalists emerged in the Jewish community. When Ezra and Nehemiah led a group of Judeans back from Babylonia to Judea, with the permission of the Persian king Cyrus, they found that many of the Judeans who had remained in the land had taken foreign wives, who had come down from the north and settled among them. Ezra and

Nehemiah insisted that the only way Jewish worship and ritual practices could be purified from foreign influences was to require that non-Jewish spouses, and the children of non-Jewish wives, be separated from their Jewish husbands and fathers, and return to their homelands. Many Judeans protested this edict, and their cause was taken up by the authors of the books of Ruth and Jonah in Hebrew Scriptures. The book of Ruth emphasizes the loyalty of a convert to Judaism, whose husband has been killed, and who insists on returning with her mother-in-law to Judea, there to marry her husband's next of kin and ensure the continuation of the family heritage. The book of Jonah teaches that Jews, in covenant with God, have the responsibility to bring the word of God to all peoples that they might be saved from their evil ways. This requirement that a Jew fulfill his mission to proclaim God's word and God's compassion to all nations was another strong response to the restrictive measures of Ezra and Nehemiah and to their particularism.

The conflicts between Jewish separatists and universalists became even sharper with the conquest of Judea by Alexander the Great around 300 B.C.E., and the emergence of Hellenism as a seductive factor in the cultural and religious life of the Judeans. The Hellenistic period was a period of revolution all over the world, breaking up the fixed frameworks of tribe and family, and putting in their place the will of the strong individual. Thus in Judea we note the infringement on family tradition by the High Priest, John Hyrcanus, who broke off relationships with his father and brothers in his quest for power. Such breaks with tradition involved not only individuals and their personal ambitions, but cultural and religious sympathies and antipathies as well.

It is clear, of course, that the Hellenizing movement was not suddenly recognized and confronted by the Maccabean revolt of 165 B.C.E. It had been preceded by a lengthy period during which Greek culture had become rooted among the people of Judea and in Diaspora Jewish communities as well. One of the leading figures who promoted Hellenism in Judea was Joseph the Tobiad, a wealthy tax collector around 220 B.C.E. Joseph's character manifested the basic traits typical of many Greeks of the period: immense willpower, self-confidence, and undisguised contempt for ancestral tradition. His was a world where power and money were supreme, annulling religious, national, and moral traditions. It was permissible to eat forbidden food at the king's table and to pursue Greek dancing girls, if thereby a man could gain entry to the society necessary to his career. Most Judeans succumbed to the popular body-building and sports events of the Gymnasium. They enjoyed the beauty and the sophistication of Greek culture and found it convenient to ignore the paganism of Greek worship of many gods.

In sharp contrast to the Hellenizing efforts of Joseph and his many followers was the resistance of the sons of Mattathias and their cohorts, as recorded in I and II Maccabees in the Apocrypha. Spurred to action by the placing of the figure of Antiochus Epiphanes within the Temple gates, and the requirement that every Jew passing the statue bow before it or be slain by the Syrian soldiers standing guard, the Maccabees revolted against the Syrian authority. By using the tactics of guerrilla warfare, this small band of revolutionaries succeeded in driving the Syrians out of Jerusalem. Though their military victory was short-lived (the Syrians recaptured Jerusalem within a year), the brief triumph of the Maccabees had great significance. Never again did the Syrians attempt to impose statues of gods and the worship of the emperor on the Judeans.

The impact of Hellenism on Judaism has been profound, even into the twentieth century. Like the Maccabees, there are always zealots who choose to isolate their communities from the impact of other cultures. They believe, as did the Maccabees, that Jewish survival depends on strict observance of the laws of Torah and resistance to any ideas or practices that might distract observant Jews from their ancient traditions. On the other hand, many Jews throughout the centuries have tried to synthesize Jewish culture with that of surrounding peoples. The foremost exponent of this approach was Philo of Alexandria. Philo dedicated much of his literary effort to validating his thesis that Hebrew Scriptures allegorically taught the basic philosophy of the Greeks. For Philo, Judaism and Hellenism were completely compatible. The danger of Maccabean isolation is stultification of intellectual and spiritual growth. The danger of Philo's pluralism is assimilation. Most contemporary Jewish leaders seek a satisfactory middle road for their followers.

At the same time that the struggle over Hellenism was taking place in Judea, there emerged three parties in Jewish life that had both political and religious philosophies: the Sadducees, the Pharisees, and the Essenes. The Sadducees were primarily the high priestly group and the more affluent Judeans. They maintained the centrality of Temple worship and literal adherence to Torah as the core of Jewish life. The Sadducees also believed that the survival of their prestige and power, and of the Temple itself, depended on their retaining good relationships with the ruling power, be it Syria or Rome, and accepting some aspects of Hellenistic civilization. The Pharisees were dissenters who refused to accept the authority of the priesthood or the centrality of the Temple. The Pharisees believed that Torah, and the study and interpretation of God's Law, was the focal point in Jewish life. Many schools, led by rabbis who were teachers and interpreters of Torah, sought to expand their understanding of Torah and its application to the problems of daily life. They developed synagogues, which were small institutions in contrast to the Temple in Jerusalem, where Jews gathered throughout Judea to worship, to study, and to maintain fellowship. The Pharisees and their way of life were virtually untouched by the impact of Hellenism on Judea. The third group, the Essenes, were members of small ascetic communities. These communities were formed primarily by priests who dissented from the authority of the high priesthood. The Essenes had no political ambitions but were content to be left alone to study and to lead a monastic life. There may have been a fourth sect known as Zealots. If such a group was formally organized, it had as its primary reason for existence the revolutionary overthrow of Roman authority in Judea.

The Sadducees disappeared with the fall of the Temple and the overthrow of Judea as a semi-independent state in 70 C.E. The Essene communities probably disappeared shortly thereafter. If there was a Zealot group, some segment of it may have survived for the last stand against Rome about 135 C.E. The Pharisees alone survived in the Diaspora, establishing synagogues and schools for study of Torah. This resulted in the development of rabbinic

Judaism, which gave to the Jewish people the codified oral Law, first in the Mishnah, edited by Judah ha-Nasi in 200 c.e., and then the Gemara, combined with the Mishnah by Ashi in 500 c.e. to form the Talmud. It was the Torah (written Law) and the Talmud (oral Law) that enabled Jews to survive the destruction of the Temple and the nation, both as a remnant in Palestine and in communities throughout the Diaspora.

Paralleling the development of rabbinic Judaism, there emerged another sect of Jews who accepted Jesus of Nazareth as the long anticipated and hoped for Messiah. A small group within the Jewish community at first, these followers of Jesus began seeking and accepting proselytes from the pagan world, as had the Jews for centuries before. Under the leadership of another Jew, Paul, they separated themselves from the established Jewish community, primarily because of the differences over ritual practices and rejection of the dietary laws of Torah. These differences were coupled with their conviction that Jesus was not only their teacher, but also their messiah and resurrected savior. Some scholars believe that competition for converts further widened the breach between Jews and the early Christians, and that this rivalry continued until about 330 c.e., when the Roman emperor Constantine established Christianity as the official religion of the Roman empire. At that time, Constantine severely limited the religious and civil rights of Jews and other minorities within the empire. This was the beginning of the restrictions on Jewish rights in Christian, and later Muslim, lands that extended through the Middle Ages to the modern period of emancipation. Moreover, with the dissemination and study of the New Testament writings, especially the Gospels, there arose the deicide charges against the Jews and the beginning of religiously oriented anti-Semitism. The accusation that Jews were Christ-killers became a dominant theme in the church's "war" against the Jews. It increased in intensity in the Middle Ages and became justification for pogroms and deprivation of Jewish civil and political rights in many European nations.

Exactly where the Middle Ages begin and end for the Jewish people is difficult to ascertain. The medieval age in general history does not necessarily coincide with the medieval age in Jewish history. The medieval epoch in Jewish life probably began with the reign of Constantine and the enactment of disabling laws against the Jews, reducing them to the status of second-class citizens. From that time until the medieval age came to an end for western European Jewry with the proclamation of political and civil emancipation in France in 1791, Jews were rarely more than a tolerated minority suffering political and social disabilities at one time or another in most lands. In addition to the religious factor, economic crises that affected royalty and peasants alike fanned the flames of anti-Semitism. The Crusades provide an excellent example of the way in which both economic and religious factors were the basis for pogroms against the Jewish ghettoes. Though the goal of the Crusades was rescue of the Holy Land from heathen hands, the crusaders' conquests were of the defenseless ghettoes, which they plundered and looted while slaughtering thousands of Jews in the name of the church.

Exile of the Jews from England (1290), France (1394), and Spain (1492), came after Jewish bankers and merchants had been bled of all their resources by the kings and then were banished, at the urging of the established church in each country, because the Jews resisted conversion to Christianity. In other lands, at the insistence of church authorities, the scope of Jewish citizenship was limited. In Christian empires, Jews could not hold high office, receive honors according to rank, or exercise any authority over Christians. The church saw to it that the Jews did not regain equality even when readmitted to their former homelands. Most importantly, the medieval popes found that they could not protect from violence those whom they proclaimed the fitting objects of oppression and contempt. Thus the church was directly responsible for the decline in the status of the Jew in most of medieval Europe.

It is not possible to answer here all of the accusations made by church leaders against the Jews. The blood accusation is but one example. From the middle of the thirteenth century to the end of the nineteenth century, there were numerous cases throughout Europe in which Jews were accused of kidnapping Christians in order to kill them and use their blood for ritual purposes. There was never a grain of truth in such charges, because nowhere in Jewish tradition was the blood of human beings used in any ritual act. The accusations gained credence, however, because they were often brought to the public by respected church officials.

By the same token, the resentment against Jewish money-lenders was instigated by bankrupt monarchs who were unable to repay loans proffered by Jewish bankers when no other source for economic survival of the nation was available. While it is no doubt true that some Jewish moneylenders were usurers and took advantage of the plights of their debtors, the tragedy was that entire Jewish communities suffered grievously because of isolated examples of individual Jews' deviation from legitimate business practices.

The breach in Jewish-Christian relationships widened appreciably in the Middle Ages. Jews learned from bitter experiences that they could not trust the Christian church hierarchy or Christian secular rulers, much less their followers. This distrust continued into the modern era, even in America, where the memories of first-generation American Jews, newly arrived from Europe, brought fresh recollections of slander and murder, too often in the name of the church. Just as it has been a difficult task to rid Christians of inherited prejudices, it has been equally difficult to help Jews blot out memories of bitter hatred and persecution.

The coming of democracy in western Europe and in America in the modern period did afford opportunities for rapprochement between Jews and Christians. The readmittance of Jews to England in the mid-seventeenth century, and the extension of civil and political rights to Jews in France's late eighteenth-century democracy, enabled Jews and Christians to begin the long, slow process of building mutual understanding and respect. It was in the United States, however, that Jews found the greatest opportunity to establish themselves as citizens, enjoying the freedom for which they had yearned for centuries.

Even in this New World, however, liberty and equality did not come easily, nor was it to be taken for granted. The first Jews to arrive in 1654 in New Amsterdam, after the long arm of the Inquisition had forced them to flee from their refuge in Brazil, were not welcomed with open arms by Peter Stuyvesant, the governor. They would not have been allowed to remain in the colony had it not been for the intervention of Jews who were stockholders in the parent Dutch West Indies Company. Though the Jews were allowed to remain, they were not granted full civil rights in New Amsterdam until one of the early settlers, Asser Levy, won a court battle to be allowed to take his turn as a guard for the colony, rather than pay a special tax that would exempt him from service because he was a Jew. Similar disabilities were experienced by Jews in most of the other colonies. In Rhode Island, Roger Williams, who himself was forced to leave the Massachusetts Bay colony in order to find religious freedom, first extended that freedom of worship to Jews. The last restrictions on Jews' political and civil rights were not finally eliminated from state constitutions until the Maryland legislature repealed its discriminatory laws in the mid-nineteenth century.

The Jewish population in the United States grew from a few thousand at the beginning of the nineteenth century to almost a half million fifty years later. As the newcomers during this period, the German Jews moved into the Midwest and the South. They encountered hostility, especially from rural fundamentalist Protestants who had never known a Jew. These Christians heard anti-Semitic diatribes from their pulpits, especially in the Easter season when the old Christ-killer charges emerged from the Gospel accounts of the trial and crucifixion of Jesus. Still greater tensions attended the arrival of almost four million Jews fleeing persecution in Eastern Europe and finding a haven of refuge in the urban East between 1880 and 1910. These tensions resulted primarily from economic concerns among some blue-collar workers and from management-labor conflicts in industry. The first major anti-Semitic outbreak in the United States developed in the Depression of the 1930s. For many years Father Coughlin taught anti-Semitism on his Sunday radio broadcasts from Detroit before he was finally silenced by the bishop of that Catholic diocese. Henry Ford's *Dearborn Independent* newspaper published the scurrilous "Protocols of Zion," which purported to reveal plans for an international conspiracy to control the world economy. In the South and the Midwest the Ku Klux Klan, with the passive acquiescence of some law enforcement officers and some "good citizens" in many communities, marched in their cloaked anonymity and burned fiery crosses on the lawns of Blacks and Jews. Most Christian leaders in the United States were passive as minorities were threatened with the same persecutions they had known in the old country. Finally, in the 1930s, the National Conference of Christians and Jews was called into being to counteract discrimination against Jews and to establish educational programs to improve relationships between Christians and Jews. The N.C.C.J. did make progress in creating an environment in which Jews and Christians could meet on common ground.

Some of the racial and religious barriers began to fall as Blacks and Whites, Christians and Jews, rubbed shoulders in the armed services, facing the common enemy in fascist Germany. Not until the full impact of the Nazi Holocaust confronted the world at the end of the Second World War, however, did some Christians begin to assess their responsibility for allowing the atrocities that resulted in six million Jews dead in concentration camps and gas chambers. The stark reality of this inhumanity awakened many church leaders to their obligation for overcoming the bitter hatred that was engendered in Hitler's Europe. The most significant and courageous step was taken by Pope John XXIII in calling for Vatican Council II, which was charged, along with many other issues, to determine how to overcome anti-Semitism both in the Catholic Church and in the larger community. Many Protestant denominations followed the lead of Vatican Council II in issuing resolutions opposing anti-Semitism and urging positive programs to overcome prejudice through education and by eradicating economic, political, and social discrimination.

Significant progress was made in eliminating barriers between Christians and Jews in the middle of the twentieth century. That progress came to a sudden halt in 1967, though, when the young State of Israel was threatened by a new attempt at genocide by seven Arab states. The Christian community in America remained strangely silent, and no material or verbal support was offered by the churches or their clergy. After Israel miraculously defeated its enemies in the Six Day War, American Jews expressed their bitter disappointment at the silence of the Christian community, and the gap between Jews and Christians widened once again. Some liberal Christian leaders have sought diligently to close that gap. Positive programs of visitations to Israel and of maintaining an awareness of the magnitude of the Holocaust tragedy in its assault on the moral fiber of all human beings have borne fruit. The formation of new Jewish-Christian alliances in common educational programs, and in facing together the urgent need for extension of civil rights and the tragic specter of hunger and homelessness in America, has once again brought Jews and Christians closer together.

HISTORICAL PERSPECTIVES ON THE RELATIONSHIPS OF JEWS AND NON-JEWS

A Christian Outlook

Christianity appeared as a branch of Judaism at a time when the Pharisees were the dominant intellectual and spiritual force within Judaism, though the situation was volatile indeed. Within forty years of the birth of Christianity the great Jewish revolt of 66–70 C.E. would take place, with Jerusalem's Temple destroyed, much of the city ravaged, its population (including the Christian population) scattered, and the stage well set for the development of the hard lines of distinction between Judaism and Christianity that were, in various forms, to continue throughout the centuries.

The Christian community arose as the followers of Jesus, sharing their experiences of Jesus' death and resurrection from death, bound themselves into a new community awaiting the fulfillment of God's promises to the people of Israel. Theirs was a Jewish hope, and their view of what God was doing in and through the one whom God had raised from death to glory was couched in Jewish terms. For some decades, Christianity continued as a Jewish movement, and indeed for centuries there were to be Christians who considered themselves Jewish and Christian. Not until the emergence of a gentile Christianity at the initiative of Peter and Paul and other apostles did the situation fundamentally change: Christianity, like the Essene community that produced the Dead Sea Scrolls, was a branch or a sect of Judaism with a distinctive understanding of Jewish life and of God's future for the people of Israel.

41

In later chapters we will deal more directly with the figure of Jesus in early Christianity and with some of the tenets of Christianity. Here it is important only to underscore the point that has so frequently been overlooked in Christian history: the Christian movement appeared within Judaism, initiated by the Jew Jesus and furthered after his death by the Jewish apostles who carried on Jesus' work and way, as they understood them.

Conflicts were inevitable between the Jerusalem Jewish community that did not accept the Christian affirmations and the Jewish community that did. There were differences also between the Essenes and the Pharisees (evident in the literature that has survived from Qumran, ancient Jewish historians, and the Mishnah) and between militant Pharisees and others disposed to avoid a direct confrontation with the Roman authorities. Judaism in the first century c.e. was a highly complex reality, even though the Pharisaic outlook was destined to predominate in the work of the rabbinical schools.

As Christian thought began to develop within Judea and Galilee and then in other parts of the Mediterranean world, the conflicts with the majority Jewish community increased. The question of how actively the majority Jewish community sought to make converts among the pagans continues to be debated. Some point to the scanty but real evidence that Judaism was actively engaged in making proselytes (converts to Judaism) at this time; note, for example, the remark attributed to Jesus in the Gospel of Matthew about the eagerness with which the Pharisees sought to win converts to Judaism (Matthew 23:15). Others, however, find such evidence less compelling. They hold that as the church and the synagogue more and more went their own ways, the Jewish community left the Christian community alone and itself wished to be left alone.

Even so, there can be no doubt that the work of Peter and Paul and other apostles, which was centered first within Jewish communities and synagogues, increasingly came to be work pursued within the non-Jewish pagan world. The apostles called on the citizens of that world to forsake their idolatry and polytheism and turn to the one God of Christian (and Jewish) faith. They also invited the same pagan world to accept God's servant Jesus of Nazareth, whom God had raised from death, as the Messiah and Savior of Israel and of the peoples of the earth. Christianity more and more came to be a direct challenge to Judaism, though it began as a movement or sect within Judaism and continued to present the Christian message in Jewish terms even to pagans.

By 66 C.E., a revolt against Rome had broken out in Galilee and Judea. Many Jewish leaders sought to prevent the spread of rebellion against Roman authority, but to no avail. The Romans had gone too far, and many of the Zealots were convinced that they were doing the will of God. The revolt was severely crushed in Jerusalem and Judea and then came to inevitable and tragic conclusion as the remnant of the Jewish opposition died in the stronghold of Masada, dying at their own hands in 74 C.E. Religious and political leadership for the Jewish community was established at the small town of Jamnia (Jabneh) near Jaffa on the coast of the Mediterranean, while some Christians pulled out of the conflict and settled at Pella in Transjordan, a few miles north of the Jabbok River.

The conflict between the majority Jewish community and the minority Christian movement in Palestine intensified in cities and towns within which the Christian movement was growing, and at a time when, within Judaism, stirrings against Rome continued. The Gospels were probably produced within Hellenistic cities and for particular Christian communities where many Jews were present. Each of the Gospels reflects, among many other things, the character of relations between the Jewish and the Christian community of the locality. The Gospel of Mark probably reveals the fact that Christianity developed in Rome in such a way as to benefit from the fact that Judaism was a recognized religion within the Roman empire. Christianity benefited from the status of its sister religion, and the Gospel of Mark does not draw the contrast between the two religions nearly so sharply as do the other Gospels. The Gospel of Matthew was addressed to a Christian community made up largely of converts to Christianity from Judaism; hence its strong representation of Jesus as the giver of a new Torah, a new divine Law. The Gospel of Luke and the companion Book of Acts give a quite sympathetic picture of the Hellenistic/Roman world and present the Jews as the chief troublemakers, while the gospel was spreading throughout the

43

Mediterranean world. The Gospel of John probably developed in stages, showing the very sharp hostilities that existed between those Jews who were accepting Christianity and those who were not. This Gospel shows very striking influences from the Hellenistic religious world, with its sharp contrasts between light and darkness, this world and the world to come, good and evil. In addition, the Gospel reflects some features of the sharp partisanship characteristic of the community that produced the Dead Sea Scrolls. In some respects, this Gospel is the most anti-Jewish of the four.

With the Jewish revolt of 132–135 c.e., led by Simeon ben Kozibah, or bar Kokhba, and supported by major leaders within the Jewish community, the situation of the Jews within the Roman empire was considerably worsened. This revolt came about because of two measures taken by the emperor Hadrian: the prohibition of the rite of circumcision throughout the empire, and the decision to rebuild the city of Jerusalem with a temple to the god Zeus atop its citadel. That was too much for the Jewish faithful.

Christianity had been persecuted to some extent under Nero in the 60s and under Domitian in the 90s of the first century c.e. The Jewish revolts of 66–70 and 132–135 c.e. had made the Roman authorities very suspicious indeed of Judaism in Palestine and somewhat suspicious of Judaism in other parts of the empire. So neither Christianity nor Judaism was in high favor within the Roman world. But Judaism did not lose its position as a religious community recognized by Rome. Christianity was considered, from time to time, as the more dangerous community, suffering at the hands of Rome on several occasions in the second and third centuries c.e. But even when it was under suspicion from Rome, the Christian community in some heavily populated Jewish areas of the Mediterranean world showed hostility to Judaism.

The cause for such hostility is, in general, not hard to find. We have outlined in chapter 1 some of the ways in which Christianity developed over against Judaism: the Hebrew Scriptures were the "Old" Testament of the Christians, their message fulfilled (and often said to be superseded) in the New Testament. Israel's failures to live up to God's covenant demands—so some Christians claimed—marked that community's witness as a failure; God had accordingly chosen the Christian community as the New Israel. Slowly the message of the Christian community developed, put together from the letters of Paul and the other apostles and from the teaching and preaching within the Christian congregations—partly affirming Judaism and partly drawing the contrast between Judaism and Christianity too sharply and too strongly. Paul's contrast between law and grace; the Gospel contrasts between the scribes and the Pharisees, on the one side, and Jesus and his followers, on the other; and the whole stress upon promise and fulfillment, with the Jewish people being the people of the promise and the Christian community the community of fulfillment—these sharp contrasts worked to heighten the tension between the Jewish and the Christian communities during the period from Jesus' death until the establishing of Christianity as the official religion of the Roman empire under Constantine in the early fourth century c.e.

Some of the great theologians of the church during this period provided many of the working formulas for the relating of Judaism and Christianity. This story has been told frequently in recent decades. Much of the polemics against the Jewish people was a part of the preaching and teaching of the Christian community, not necessarily intended to be broadcast to the world at large and not directly addressed to the Jewish community. It is important to recognize that during much of the period after 135 c.e., the Jewish communities of the Mediterranean world simply went their own ways and ignored their Christian counterpart. Only occasionally were there direct and vocal Christian attacks in public upon the Jewish people prior to the establishment of Christianity as the religion of the empire. Within the Christian community, however, it was found expedient to show the sharp contrast between Judaism and the new religion, always to the disparagement of Judaism. So long as the Christian community had to make its own way in the Roman world as a new and much challenged religious force, it was not in a position to make public denunciations of Judaism a part of its regular message; in fact, Judaism and Christianity in many parts of the empire were careful not to become too vocal a political force at all, for fear of doing their cause harm. Even so, Christianity was clearly developing its message in sharp contrast to Judaism, and the seeds for more violent assaults upon the Jewish people were being sown as Christian theology developed in the Mediterranean world prior to the establishment of Christianity as the religion of the empire.

From the Establishment to the Late Renaissance

Under Constantine and his successors Christianity had the place of ascendancy while Judaism continued to be a recognized religion, although subjected to many discriminatory acts by the Christian authorities. Christianity, as the established religion of the state, spread rapidly in some areas but was stopped in others as peoples pushed into the West from eastern Europe and western Asia. But Christianity often gained great allegiance among the so-called barbarians, and continued to be the dominant force as the remainder of Europe was incorporated into the Christian world. As the dominant religious reality, Christianity more and more came to view itself as the rightful heir of the heritage of Israel, to the detriment of the Jewish community. At the very best, Judaism was considered a religion inferior to Christianity.

With the coming of Islam in the early seventh century, both Judaism and Christianity suffered considerably in some lands. In the course of time, both communities were able to establish some place for themselves within the Islamic territories, although Christianity, as the religion of the chief enemy of Islam in Europe, was viewed with the greater suspicion by the Muslim world.

Classical medieval Christian thought continued to treat Judaism as an inferior religious position. It had no difficulty in justifying the mistreatment of Jews—individual Jews and the Jewish community as a whole. Particularly malevolent charges were leveled against the Jews, the most vicious being that they engaged in human sacrifice, especially in connection with the Passover ceremony. Such calumnies developed in many European lands, leading to the final act of expulsion of the Jews from several of them. Similar charges had been leveled against the Christians in early times. But there were distinguished Jews in several European countries who were on good terms with their

Christian neighbors and were widely respected for their qualities and their writings and other accomplishments. The grim truth is, however, that European Christianity systematically mistreated the Jewish people throughout this entire period. Jews were expelled from Britain in the thirteenth century, from France in the fourteenth century, and from Spain in the late fifteenth century. Even the greatest of the church's theologians of medieval times did not break through the wall of Christian prejudice against Judaism.

From the Reformation to the Enlightenment

With the work of the German reformer Martin Luther, Christianity entered upon a new stage of relations with Judaism. On the one hand, the Hebrew Scriptures had in Luther one of their brilliant interpreters. His sermons, commentaries, and his magnificent translation of the Hebrew Bible brought fresh appreciation of the heritage of the Jewish people and planted that appreciation firmly in the life of the church. On the other hand, Luther's determination to concentrate only on "that which pertains to Christ" in his interpretation of the Hebrew Bible, and his polemical and sometimes vicious words of condemnation of the Jews, added a fresh chapter to Christian mistreatment of the Jewish people. Luther's genius assured that his followers would not forget what he had to say about the Hebrew Bible and about the Jews.

The other Reformers were less polemical and violent in what they said about the Jews. John Calvin's detailed commentaries on the Bible display his careful exegetical study of the biblical texts. His strong emphasis on the place of the law in the Christian life and in society also meant that his theological appreciation of the continuing value of the Hebrew Scriptures was much higher than that of other Reformers.

In the Counter-Reformation and in the further expansion of Reformation thought, the Hebrew Scriptures continued to exercise strong influence in the Christian states of Europe. The theory of divine kingship, for example, drew heavily from the place attributed to kingship in the Hebrew Bible. Even so, the dominant position within the Christian community continued to be to treat Judaism as an inferior religion, and indeed an outmoded one. Christianity was the successor religion; why would the Jews not recognize that fact?

From the Enlightenment to the Present

With the coming of the Enlightenment and the emergence in Europe of liberal democratic thought, the attitude of Christian Europe toward the Jews changed considerably. Whether the states continued to recognize Christianity as the established religion or withdrew such recognition (as in France), acknowledgment of the right of the Jews to live in peace with their neighbors came to be widespread. Jews were permitted to return to all European lands, and their rights as citizens were slowly recognized throughout Europe. In the course of time, many Jews joined the Christian community, or simply laid aside any practices that maintained their identification as Jews. The majority of the Jewish population, clearly, continued to recognize that Jews remained second-class citizens in Christian or in secular Europe.

There emerged, however, in mid-nineteenth-century Europe formal assaults against the Jewish people as such, attacking their very right to citizenship and to a place within the western democratic states. The charge was that Jews were a corrupting influence within the society, either by their controlling the flow of wealth and ideas and using these to their own selfish advantage or by their undermining the moral foundation of western Christian society. Long before Adolf Hitler, programmatic anti-Semitism arose in western European lands, in particular in Germany and France. Such charges came to their obscene climax in the National Socialist movement in Germany.

Anti-Semitism and Christian misunderstanding of Judaism in Europe and elsewhere in the world clearly made it possible for National Socialism to proceed unchecked for years. Its commitment was nothing less than to rid the world of the Jewish people. We will be dealing with the Holocaust later in this book; at this point it need only be said that the nadir of relations between Judaism and Christianity came with Hitler's program to exterminate the Jewish people as such—the so-called final solution.

The Jews in North America

Jews found their way to the New World very early. Congregations were established in New England, in the Caribbean, and in the South already in the seventeenth century. They had a hand in shaping the doctrine of the separation of church and state at the time of the framing of the United States Constitution and the Bill of Rights. From early times, Jews in the United States and Canada came to be viewed less as objects of conversion or assimilation than as neighbors with their own religious traditions deserving of respect.

Jewish immigrants increased to such an extent that the Jewish community had a strong base from which to respond to acts of hostility and discrimination. Moreover, Jewish participation in political and social life in Canada and the United States was intense; by the beginning of the twentieth century such active political, social, and cultural leadership had given a high standing indeed to the Jewish communities in most large cities of North America. Even so, many forms of discrimination against the Jews continued, and Christian misunderstandings and ignorance played their part in such discrimination.

During the twentieth century, relations between Jews and Christians have undergone a revolution. Especially since the Holocaust and the end of the Second World War, continuing efforts on the part of Jews and Christians have produced radical changes in the ways in which Christians describe the Jewish people in their church school literature. Discrimination against Jews in education, government, business, and industry has not been eliminated, but it has been radically curtailed. What remains, as noted above, is the urgent need on the part of the church to grant that Judaism has its continuing validity as a religion alongside Christianity, and that the continuing existence of Judaism is not only not a threat to Christianity but rather a good thing for the health of both and for the health of the society as a whole.

In other lands, too, this recognition is spreading, even in those countries in which Christianity is the established religion. But millions of Christians the world over still have not come to such a recognition—and thus serious exchanges between the two communities continue to be essential and urgent. Even after the Holocaust, in which the Christian community was so deeply implicated, and after the establishment of the State of Israel, there remains a massive task of education within the Christian communities of the world.

This brief sketch can conclude with a reminder that there has been one central reason for Christian mistreatment of the Jewish people. Christianity relates to Judaism as it does to no other world religion. It is dependent upon Israel for its sacred history, for its Scripture, for its moral guidelines and foundation in the divine law, and for much of its fundamental theology and its ethics. Christianity has not often been ready to accept its task as that of presenting the God of Israel, as known centrally in Jesus the Christ, to the non-Jewish world, while counting upon Israel to continue to live in covenant with God and to display before the world what it means to be God's covenant people. The Christian community has found it almost irresistible to interpret its life and mission in such a way as to eliminate the need for, or even the place of, a continuing Jewish faith and witness. The chief cause of Christian mistreatment of the Jewish people lies there: The right thing for Jews to do—Christians have claimed—is to convert to Christianity; if they will not, they must be particularly stubborn or blind or clannish or (worst of all) under a divine curse.

In subsequent chapters we shall attempt to sort out what can be done to relate Christianity and Judaism to each other in ways that offer hope of overcoming the hostilities that have developed over the centuries. Much of what we say will be a reporting on important developments in recent decades that lead in that direction. We hope to have additional insights and suggestions that can make the dialogue more fruitful still.

Suggested Readings

Bokser, B. Z. *Judaism and the Christian Predicament.*
Lohse, E. *The New Testament Environment.*
Neusner, J. *Judaism and Christianity.*
―――. *From Politics to Piety: The Emergence of Pharisaic Judaism.*
Odeberg, H. *Pharisaism and Christianity.*
Parkes, J. *The Conflict of the Church and the Synagogue.*
Rivkin, E. *A Hidden Revolution.*
Rogow, A. *The Jew in a Gentile World.*
Sandmel, S. *Judaism and Christian Beginnings.*
Simon, M. *Verus Israel.*
Tcherikover, V. *Hellenistic Civilization and the Jews.*
Thoma, C. *A Christian Theology of Judaism.*

CHAPTER THREE

UNDERSTANDING OUR SCRIPTURES

A Jewish Outlook

Jews have been known as "the people of the Book" throughout the centuries. The Book, or Hebrew Scriptures, records the history of our people from the first Jew, Abraham, through our people's re-establishment of the Torah in Jerusalem and the restoration of the walled city under the leadership of Ezra and Nehemiah. This covers more than eleven hundred years of a developing relationship between the Jewish people and their God, highlighted by a series of covenants in which God promised to protect them and to establish them in a fertile land if the people truly accepted Yahweh as their God alone, and served their God by living according to the moral law Yahweh gave to Moses at Sinai.

The Book, however, is far more than history. The thirty-nine books that are included in this monumental anthology raise some of the most profound theological and philosophical questions ever to confront humankind. Through these books we are challenged and chastised as our people seek to live according to God's ethical principles, or attempt to evade God's watchful eye. We find within the books of the Hebrew Scriptures a deepening sense of the joy of life, comfort in facing life's sorrows, and guidance in the eternal quest for the meaning and purpose of our lives.

We are, moreover, "the people of the Book" not only because we seek to live by its teachings, but because we accept the mission to transmit it to all the children of God. The text has been translated into more languages than has that of any other book ever written. The Book is sacred to Christians and Muslims, as well as Jews.

It is important that we understand that the thirty-nine books in Hebrew Scriptures are exactly the same thirty-nine books that Christians refer to as the Old Testament. The books are arranged in a different sequence in the two traditions, though the order is the same, in both the Jewish and Christian editions, for the first five books: Genesis, Exodus, Leviticus, Numbers, and Deuteronomy. These books are known to Jews as the Torah, and to Christians as the Pentateuch. The remaining books are arranged quite differently in the Christian canon, with the Old Testament following primarily a historical sequence, and the Hebrew Scriptures categorized according to subject matter as well as by a historical pattern.

The second division of Hebrew Scriptures is called Prophets. It contains historical prophetic writings: Joshua, Judges, I and II Samuel, and I and II Kings. The division also includes the literary prophets, known as the major and minor prophets. The difference between major and minor prophets has nothing to do with which book is more important. The terms simply denote the quantity of the extant manuscripts of the particular prophet. The three largest books are the major prophetic writings: Isaiah, Jeremiah, and Ezekiel. Then follow the twelve minor prophets, some as brief as a chapter or two.

The third division of our Hebrew Bible is called Sacred Writings. This is the section that contains the poetry of the Psalms and Song of Songs, as well as the wisdom literature: Proverbs, Job, and Ecclesiastes. There are thirteen books included in the Sacred Writings.

The other important difference between the books found in both the Hebrew Scriptures and the Old Testament is in the translation of some of the texts. The oldest extant manuscript of Hebrew Scriptures is the Masoretic text, in which a group of Jewish scholars added vowels and punctuation marks to an earlier text. Many of the Christian translations of the Old Testament, on the other hand, are based on the Septuagint, a Greek translation of Hebrew manuscripts thought to have been more ancient than the Masoretic text. There can be considerable difference in translations of words into English from the Hebrew and Greek texts. This leads to some significant differences in interpretation of certain passages, and it is one of the things that make the study of Scripture so fascinating. For example, in the book of Isaiah most scholars translate the word "almah" from the Hebrew as "young woman." Many of the translations from the Greek, however, record the Greek translation of the Hebrew as "virgin" in English. This ultimately affects the story of the birth of Jesus and his parenthood. It becomes tremendously important in determining whether we view Jesus as inspired prophet or teacher or as a divine being.

Likewise, there is considerable difference in interpretation when Jews and Christians study the later chapters of the book of Isaiah, especially the passages concerned with messianic expectations. The ways in which we interpret the book of Isaiah have a great deal to do with how we view Jesus as Christ, or Messiah, who has come or is yet to be. We shall discuss this in greater depth in chapter 5, "Understanding Our Relationship to Jesus."

Torah/Pentateuch

The moral laws of Torah are the foundation upon which all the rest of the teachings in Hebrew Scriptures are based. Furthermore, Torah provides both the motivation and the guidance for leading a Jewish life. It is important, then, that we understand what we mean by the word *Torah*.

Within the Jewish community, Orthodox and Reform Jews differ in defining Torah. Orthodox Jews accept Torah as "Law," as that which was given in complete and final form to Moses at Sinai. Therefore, since Torah was God's absolute revelation, Orthodox Jews must follow as literally as possible all the moral teachings and ritual practices found in these five books.

Reform Jews prefer the translation of Torah as "instruction." We believe that in all probability Torah was written by many men over several hundred years. There were at least four schools of writers, which the German scholar Wellhausen called J, E, P, and D. J and E differed, for example, in the word used for God in their scrolls, the J school using the word *Jehovah* or *Yahweh* for God, and the E school using the word *Elohim* for God. The P school represents the contributions of the priestly community,

55

primarily regulations for ritual practices. The D school contributed most of the book of Deuteronomy, found in the Temple by the Prophetess Huldah about the year 621 B.C.E.

For Reform Jews, Torah is instruction from God-inspired men and women from around 800 to 450 B.C.E. This dating is based primarily on the book of Nehemiah, where we learn that the first time Torah was read in public was following the restoration of the second Temple. Monday and Thursday mornings, when the farmers brought their produce into Jerusalem from the surrounding countryside, and on Saturday at the Sabbath service, Ezra read and interpreted Torah both in Hebrew and in Aramaic translation.

What, then, is Torah? Torah is history, beginning perhaps with Abraham and continuing to the death of Moses. It is also midrash, a Hebrew term that refers to the act of interpreting Torah, discerning its moral teachings and ethical principles. The more we plumb the depths of Torah study, though, the more we are challenged by its profundity of thought, as well as by perplexing questions for whose answers we are still searching.

The history, folklore, and moral instruction that we find in Torah are important, but they are not reason enough for the place of reverence that Torah occupies in Jewish life. When we speak of Torah, we not only speak of the first five books in our Hebrew Scriptures, we also speak of sacred scrolls. Those of you who have visited a temple or synagogue know that in the center of the back wall of the pulpit there is an ark. When the holy ark is opened, you see a number of scrolls, each containing the same first five books of Hebrew Scriptures. From these scrolls we read on the Sabbath as part of the scriptural lesson that is incorporated into our worship experience. Torah is the resource for our study of God's word during our worship on Sabbaths and holidays. Torah is also the basis for ritual and dietary laws and for sacrificial worship. Though there has been no sacrificial worship in Jewish life since the destruction of the second Temple in 70 C.E., the worship experience and the significance of the variety of reasons for sacrifices had an impact on future liturgical development.

If all this is not enough reason for the Torah's being so central in Jewish life, Torah is most importantly a record of the development of a covenantal relationship between God and Israel. It begins with the covenant with Noah, symbolized by the rainbow, which is a reminder of God's promise never again to destroy the earth and its inhabitants by flood. Next come the covenants with Abraham: the covenant of circumcision and the covenant of the land. Torah reaches climactic heights in the covenant with Moses, symbolized by the Ten Commandments. This is the intentional import of Torah in Jewish life.

The Prophets

The prophetic books, which form the second division of Hebrew Scriptures, seek to apply the teachings of Torah to the lives of the people. A prophet was thought to be a person called by God to speak the word of God, as the prophet felt it revealed to him. From Samuel, in the books of Samuel, through Elijah and Elisha in the books of Kings, and then the fifteen literary prophets, these messengers revealed God's anger and love, God's justice and mercy, to a people floundering in their efforts to maintain a covenantal relationship with their God.

The messages of the literary prophets were profoundly influenced by the times in which they lived: pre-exilic (800–586 B.C.E.), exilic (586–516 B.C.E.), and post-exilic (516–250 B.C.E.). Most of us think of the pre-exilic prophets as great castigators of their people. Hosea and Amos, First Isaiah and Micah, preached before the destruction of the northern kingdom of Israel (721 B.C.E.). The essence of their message was that Israel, and later Judah, would be destroyed as free nations because of two basic transgressions.

The first transgression against which the pre-exilic prophets inveighed was the people's disloyalty to the one God. Although the Israelites brought their sacrifices to Yahweh in the promised land, they also brought sacrificial offerings to other gods in order to be certain that they would have the blessing and protection of whatever gods might still exercise power in that land. As might be expected, the prophets warned that God would not retain a covenant with the Hebrews if they violated their part of the covenant by worshiping other gods along with Yahweh.

The second transgression was in their relationships with one another, individually and as communities. Because they did not live in harmony as brothers and sisters, they would lose that which they could have retained had they been a unified community sharing equitably the bounty that God had provided. The prophets always offered the hope that the people would turn from their sinful ways and that God would forgive them. The pre-exilic prophets, however, did not expect this to occur.

The writings of Jeremiah, an exilic prophet, and of the post-exilic prophets Second and Third Isaiah (the authors of all or parts of Isaiah chapters 40–55 and 56–66), Ezekiel, and others present an entirely different message. There was no point in castigating the Israelites and the Judeans when the earlier prophecy had been fulfilled and they had lost their land and their liberty. The exilic and post-exilic prophets came with a message of comfort and of hope. The hope was that there would be a renewal of the covenant, and that there would again be a messianic figure who would help them return to their land in freedom and in peace.

This term "messiah," as Jews interpret its use in prophetic teachings, is crucial to an understanding of the ultimate end of time envisioned by authors of many of the books in Hebrew Scriptures. The word "messiah" comes from the Hebrew "mashiach" and is translated "anointed one." We learn of the "anointed one" first in the books of Samuel. The prophet Samuel was asked by the twelve tribes, after they had settled in their promised land, to appoint for them a king. They had found that they could not exist as twelve independent tribes because there were too many other nations that had previously occupied this fertile land or had wanted to occupy it, who were challenging their right to be there.

The only way those Hebrew tribes could defend their land was to unify under one leader. But every tribe had its own judge or leader, and these men and women were reluctant to give way, one for the other. Finally they decided that they would turn to Samuel, who came out of a priestly background, and ask him to appoint or designate a king for them. Samuel was reluctant to do this, because he was afraid a king would interfere with the people's recognition of their primary dependency on God as their Supreme Leader. Samuel understood, however, the practical necessity of having a unified nation to defend their land. Therefore he announced that he would not choose a king, but he would ask God to give him a sign as to who should be king if, indeed, there should be one.

Samuel believed that he received a message from God to choose Saul to be the first king of the Hebrew nation. He then assembled the leaders of all the tribes, and in their presence anointed Saul as the first king. The same pattern was followed when Saul could no longer carry the burden of leadership. David was anointed by Samuel to be the second king of the nation. Solomon was anointed by the priest Zadok when he became the third king designated to help preserve the promised land that God had given as part of his covenantal relationship.

Later in Israel's and Judea's histories, when these nations were conquered by mighty empires, when the people yearned for freedom and for the opportunity to live in peace under their own rulers, they prayed that God would designate still another "mashiach," who would be God's instrument to bring the people to an era of freedom and peace in their land. This was the hope that sustained the Judeans after they were conquered and their Temple destroyed by Babylon. The Jews who remained in Judea as a remnant looked forward to a restoration; those taken captive to Babylon prayed for the day of their return to the homeland. Both communities sought a messiah who would help them fulfill these aspirations.

Even more important, though, is the stress on the divine-human relationship in the messages of the prophets. Martin Buber expresses this best in his book *The Prophetic Faith*. Buber had a profound understanding of the relationship between God and human beings as interpreted by the prophets. He wrote that the relationship between God and individuals stands out in the certainty that the divine righteousness desires to continue through human righteousness, and that humanity's state depends on whether we submit to God's will or deny it. God appoints the king as God's representative over the people, in order that the king may lead justly and mercifully in God's name. The unity of justice and mercy is one of the basic concepts of the divine-human relationship in Jewish thought. We are told to imitate God and to think of a completion of God's work by human activity. This is the essence of prophetic teaching about the way in which the covenant bond between God and the Jewish people would be ultimately fulfilled.

Sacred Writings

A different aspect of our relationship with God is emphasized in Sacred Writings, the third section of Hebrew Scriptures. While the prophets were primarily concerned with the nation's holy bond with the One God and with the nation's obedience to God's moral law, the authors of the books in Sacred Writings focused on the individual's relationship with God. The Psalms, for example, are, for the most part, songs of thanksgiving and prayers of supplication. They are the best examples of earliest Jewish verbal worship. The book of Proverbs provides guidance for individual conduct, especially in relationships between parents and children. Books like Job and Ecclesiastes raise imponderable questions: Why do the righteous suffer? Does life have meaning and purpose? Though the authors do not provide final answers, they do offer patterns of thought that help us understand human suffering and frustration. Song of Songs, one of the most beautiful books in Sacred Writings, is a collection of love songs that glorify our perception of nature and sensitize us to the beauty of the intimacy that can develop in the relationship between man and woman. Each of the thirteen books of Sacred Writings offers a unique contribution to our knowledge of God and God's universe, justifying their inclusion in the total anthology of Hebrew Scriptures, known in Jewish tradition by the name "Tanakh."

The Apocrypha

The second collection of Jewish scriptural material is the Apocrypha. This anthology includes additions to some biblical books that were found after Hebrew Scriptures was completed, as well as books written later than those included in our Hebrew Bible. Many of the books of the Apocrypha were included in the Christian Bible. They are known as intertestamental books because they were placed between the Old and the New Testaments.

One of the most interesting aspects of the Apocrypha is that many of the books in the collection show a very strong influence from Hellenism. Hellenism was brought into Judea shortly before 300 B.C.E. by the Greeks under Alexander the Great. Hellenism had a decided impact on the thinking of Jewish writers of that period, but there is also material in the Apocrypha that may be dated as early as 550 B.C.E., the time of the Babylonian exile.

The Apocrypha includes supplements to the wisdom literature of Hebrew Scriptures, books like the Wisdom of Solomon and Ecclesiasticus. We also find there a continuation of Jewish history in I and II Maccabees, books that recount the struggle of the Jews to remain loyal to Yahweh at a time when the Syrian king Antiochus plundered the Temple in Jerusalem, profaned it by introducing foreign religious practices, and forbade the worship of Yahweh. First and Second Maccabees tell of the struggle for maintenance of traditional Jewish values at a time when Hellenism provided a more attractive way of life for many Judeans.

The Apocrypha also includes some noteworthy apocalyptic literature such as II Esdras. Included, too, are Susanna, the Book of the Three Holy Children, and Bel and the Dragon, all supplements to the book of Daniel. The Apocrypha, although not sacred writings for Jews because these books are not incorporated into Hebrew Scriptures, nevertheless contains important material that enables us to understand the development of new Jewish concepts about life and about the relationship of God to the Jewish people.

The Talmud

Another most important anthology of Jewish writings is the Talmud. Talmud means "learning"; this compilation of rabbinic thought contains thirty-seven tractates in six basic divisions. The content of these divisions includes: first, agricultural laws because Jews were primarily farmers when the Talmud was written, between 200 B.C.E. and 500 C.E.; second, Sabbath and Festival Laws; third, family law, emphasizing the rights of women in marriage, divorce, and inheritances; fourth, civil and criminal law and a structure for ideal government; fifth, sacrifices and other matters devoted to the Temple in Jerusalem; and sixth, rules of ritual purity and impurity.

The Talmud developed in two sections, the Mishnah and the Gemara. The first section is called Mishnah, which means "repetition." The name refers to the fact that all of Talmud was considered to be the oral law, also given to Moses at Sinai but not written down as was the Hebrew Scriptures. Therefore Talmudic law was transmitted orally from generation to generation; it could be studied and retained only through verbal repetition. The Mishnah was compiled in written form and edited by Judah ha-Nasi in about 200 C.E.

The most intriguing section of the Mishnah is a small collection known as Pirke Avot (Sayings of the Fathers). This is a compilation of profound ethical and moral truths offered by many Rabbis as guides to a more fulfilling life in relationships with God and with fellow human beings. Let me share one of these pithy sayings with you, that you may enjoy a glimpse of the wisdom of our sages.

One of the greatest of all Rabbis was Hillel, who lived shortly before Jesus and who may well have had a deep influence on Jesus' thinking. In Pirke Avot, Hillel is quoted as saying: "Separate not thyself from the congregation; trust not in thyself until the day of death; judge not thy fellowman until thou art come into his place; and say not anything which cannot be understood at once, in the hope that it will be understood in the end; neither say, when I have leisure I will study; perchance thou wilt not have leisure." Hillel is also the Rabbi who first wrote the Golden Rule that was included in the Mishnah, in a negative form: "Whatsoever is hateful unto thee, do it not unto thy fellow."

The second division of the Talmud is the Gemara, an Aramaic word meaning "learning." The Rabbis of the Gemara sought to interpret and amplify the writings in the Mishnah; therefore the Gemara is considerably larger than the Mishnah. Though the Mishnah was written in Hebrew, the Gemara is in Aramaic, each being written in the language spoken by most of the Jews at the time the different generations of Rabbis were teaching.

In discussion of Mishnaic laws, many Rabbis' interpretations of a specific law may be included by the editor of the Gemara, Rabbi

Ashi. One example will serve to illustrate the way in which the Rabbis interpreted a law in the Gemara.

A woman purchased a chicken from her kosher butcher for the family's Sabbath meal. When she returned home and began preparing the chicken, she noticed that the gall sac had been split by accident, and so according to the dietary laws the chicken was no longer kosher. Frantically the woman ran to her Rabbi to tell him of her misfortune and to ask his advice as to what she might do with the chicken. Sabbath was fast approaching, so she could not return the chicken to the butcher. The Rabbi listened to the woman's story and then reluctantly told her that since the chicken was now tainted and no longer kosher, she must dispose of it. A similar incident occurred in another community, and the second woman turned to her Rabbi for advice. He was more liberal in his interpretation of Jewish law, and so he ruled that since the woman bought the chicken in good faith as a kosher fowl, she was permitted to serve it to her family for dinner. Her intent was the important factor in this decision. A similar query came to still another Rabbi in a distant village. He presumably did not know of the rulings of the other Rabbis. This third Rabbi, therefore, had still a different solution: the parts of the chicken that had been touched by the fluid from the gall sac must be destroyed, but those portions that had not been so tainted could be served to the family.

The editor of the Gemara would then conclude the section by stating that he favored the opinion of one of the Rabbis; or by indicating that the majority of the Rabbis he consulted favored one of the rulings; or by declaring that any of the three arguments could be considered valid and therefore the student must assume the responsibility of determining which decision he felt to be the wisest and most consistent with the spirit of the Torah.

The study of the Talmud has continued through the centuries, enabling Jews living throughout the world to have guidelines as to how best to maintain their heritage. During the course of time, many Rabbis have written their own commentaries on the Talmud to aid students in their studies of the more complex and difficult passages. Most editions of the Talmud include such commentaries on both sides of the pages, as well as in notes in all the margins. Among the most famous of these rabbinic commentators were Rashi, a French Rabbi who lived in the eleventh century, and Ibn Ezra, a twelfth-century Spanish Jew.

It takes a lifetime even to scratch the surface of Talmudic study; none of us ever completes the study. For the Orthodox Jew, the introduction to Talmudic studies begins soon after he is proficient in his knowledge of Torah. These studies continue throughout the boy's formal education and into adult life, because the Talmud provides the foundation upon which his entire life pattern will be established. While Conservative and Reform Jews also study Talmud, theirs is a less intensive undertaking, because Reform and Conservative Jews are not required to follow rabbinic law unless the individual chooses to accept responsibility to live by those laws that are especially meaningful to him or her as part of a Jewish way of life. For all Jews, however, the Talmud remains, next to Hebrew Scriptures, the most important literary heritage bequeathed from generation to generation.

UNDERSTANDING OUR SCRIPTURES

A Christian Outlook

What Is Christian Scripture?

Christians sometimes forget that the only Bible Jesus had was the Jewish Bible—what Christians call the Old Testament. The New Testament had not yet been produced. But what was contained in this Jewish Bible used by the earliest Christians?

The Jewish Bible that the early Christians adopted as their own was larger than the Bible adopted by the Rabbis by about the end of the first century c.e. It was larger because it contained most of the books now found in the Apocrypha. Christians kept these apocryphal books as part of their Bible when the Rabbis decided to set them aside. In fact, there were three distinct forms of the Jewish Bible in the period when Christianity was appearing. There was one form found in Babylonia, another that was common in Egypt, and a third that appeared in Palestine. These versions of the Bible did not differ greatly among one another except for the inclusion in the Alexandrian (Egyptian) canon of the apocryphal books.

At the time of Jesus, the Jews in Palestine seem to have had knowledge of all three of these forms of the Hebrew Bible. At any rate, all three of these text traditions are found among the manuscripts and fragments of manuscripts discovered among the Dead Sea Scrolls. Most of the quotations of the "Old Testament" in the New Testament are taken from the longer, Alexandrian form of the Hebrew Bible.

The Christian Bible in the first century c.e., therefore, was the Jewish Bible, without the New Testament as yet, but with the apocryphal books that were found in the Alexandrian Jewish canon.

How the Christian Community Appropriated the Jewish Bible

Christians often have supposed that Jesus and the early Christian community were interested in the Jewish Bible only because it "prophesied" the coming of the Messiah. It is certainly true that the Hebrew Scriptures were understood to foretell the coming of Jesus of Nazareth, born of a virgin, born in Bethlehem, hailed by the nations as the Savior of humankind, but rejected by the Jewish leaders. As the early Christians put together the Gospels and collected the letters of Paul and the other apostles, they of course did so in light of their own experience of God's revelation in Jesus, and they searched the Jewish Scriptures for signs confirming that Jesus was indeed the long-awaited Messiah descended from King David.

But the Hebrew Scriptures were the guide for Jesus' daily life just as they were for other faithful Jews of his time. God's gift of the Torah, the divine Teaching, was as important to the early Christians as it was to Jews who did not accept Christianity, for it was also the rule and guide of their daily life. These Christians observed the Sabbath and the appointed festivals, and considered themselves to be heirs of Moses and the prophets. They sang and studied the Psalms and the wisdom texts.

The study of the Hebrew Scriptures in Jesus' day was becoming more and more a specialist's task. The synagogue was the house of study par excellence. Elders and other learned and devout students of Torah pursued their studies with great thoroughness and diligence, and Jesus did the same. The Dead Sea Scrolls community shows us another group that sought in the most rigorous of ways to order their lives on the basis of their devout and constant study of Torah. The purposes for the study of Torah varied from group to group, but the sacred writings were becoming more and more the object of intensive study.

Reading sacred literature is a very complex operation. One reads, in the first place, because one is convinced that there is guidance for one's life to be gained from the reading. But since times change, readers read with their own ways of understanding at work, informed by their own view of the world, and attentive to their own particular questions. Christians were reading the Hebrew Bible in light of their experience of Jesus' teaching, healings, personal qualities, suffering, death, and resurrection. Just as the Rabbis interpreted the Hebrew Scriptures in the light of their understanding of the continuing life of the Jewish people, so the early Christians read and interpreted the Jewish Bible in the light of their own lives and experiences.

Appropriating Jewish History

Several familiar ways of interpretation appear in the New Testament. The most common is what we can call *historical*. The early Christians, as well as Jesus, understood their history to be continuous with the history of Israel. What God had promised through Abraham and Moses and the prophets was finding realization in the lives of the Jewish Christians, since they were a part of that promise, and since Israel's history was theirs. Paul went to the Jewish synagogues of the Mediterranean world during his journeys because the message *for the gentiles* should be presented in a Jewish form and from a Jewish podium. The God of Israel was the Christian God. The hope of Israel was the Christian hope. The moral life to which Christians were called was the moral life that Israel's prophets and teachers and lawgivers had presented to Israel.

Updating the History of Israel

But Jews and Christians understood that the scriptures also contained guidance and meaning for later times than those in which the message had first appeared. To express this newer import for the words of the narrators, psalmists, lawgivers, and prophets, there were several modes of interpretation used by Jews and by Christians. One well documented interpretative device was simply to *assume* a further meaning, while not denying the original meaning of a text. In the Habakkuk Commentary (the Hebrew term for commentary is *pesher*) from the Dead Sea Scrolls, Habakkuk 2:4 ("the righteous shall live by faith") is interpreted as applying to the Qumran community, calling on them to place their confidence in the Teacher of Righteousness (or the Righteous Teacher) and fulfilling the demands of life in this covenant community. The meaning in Habakkuk's day is not denied, but this "updated" meaning supplements the message from the prophet Habakkuk.

A form of this type of interpretation is called "typology." Paul's use of Adam and the New Adam in I Corinthians 15 is a good example. The first man, made of dust, is the prototype of all humanity thereafter, for all are of dust and are mortal. But the Second Man, Jesus as the Christ, while also mortal and therefore belonging to humankind, to the First Adam, also is of heaven, having been raised by God to newness of life, the "firstborn of the dead." Typological interpretation appears in the Hebrew Bible as well: To the first Exodus corresponds a new Exodus (Isaiah 51:9-11, for example); to the first creation a new creation (Isaiah 65:17; 66:22).

Allegorical Interpretation

A different but related, and more problematic, kind of correspondence is *allegory*. Allegory operates on a different principle, for it, unlike typology, may have little interest at all in the original meaning of the text being used for allegorical purposes. Allegory also finds meaning in details, even minute details, while often overlooking the original meanings. The dream-visions of the book of Daniel, for example, offer all sorts of mysterious details that are clearly intended to refer to historical developments in the early second century B.C.E. The Syrian king Antiochus Epiphanes is the real enemy, not the Babylonian or Persian or early Greek enemies. The author of these Daniel visions is pointing to the great damage done by Antiochus to the Israelite people, which led to the military and political achievements of the Maccabees. The author is interested not in Babylonian and Persian history, but only in the events unfolding at the time of Antiochus' persecution and following it.

In the New Testament, Paul's use of the story of Abraham, Hagar and Sarah, and Ishmael and Isaac (Galatians 4:21-31) is an allegory about the two covenants, the Jewish and the Christian.

Paul completely ignores the fact that Hagar has no connection with Mount Sinai historically, or with Jerusalem, as he looks for ways to contrast Jews and gentiles, or law and grace.

Literary Readings

Literary forms of interpretation flourish in the Hebrew Bible and in the New Testament. The early Christians read and interpreted the Hebrew Scriptures as literature, and not only for particular religious ideas that they contained. They fed upon the poetic power and truth of biblical narratives, psalms, hymns, laments, and prophetic utterances. They gained insight and direction for their lives from the reading and study of the laws of Israel and from the wisdom traditions and their proverbs and precepts. This literary, intellectual, and spiritual heritage was the support and the guide for early Christians, even as the conflicts developed between Jews who did not accept Jesus as the Christ and Jews who did, or between Jewish Christianity and gentile Christianity.

Christian Appropriation of Hebrew Scripture

One mode of interpretation that is clearly *not* acceptable is the flat claiming of the Hebrew Scriptures as Christian Scripture exclusively. The conflicts mirrored in the New Testament show that sometimes the claim was made that what God had done for and with Israel was not for Israel's sake but for the sake of the Christian community. In assessing the adequacy of Christian use of the Hebrew Bible, a negative criterion seems to be in order. Any Christian reading of the Hebrew Bible that does not leave the message of the Hebrew Bible *for Israel* intact is inadequate or is plainly wrong. The Bible of the Jews cannot be claimed as applicable to the world *only* in the form of Christian interpretation.

The New Testament

By the end of the first century C.E., or soon thereafter, the Christian addition to the Hebrew Bible, the New Testament, was virtually complete. Its two basic parts, the Gospels and the

Apostolic Letters, had been assembled and were being copied very widely, and in book form (i.e., pieces of skin prepared for writing on both sides, cut into rectangular pieces and sewn together to form a book). How did this come about?

The Formation of the Gospels

Jesus' teachings and sayings, and stories about Jesus, were collected from the earliest times. From these, and from the expansion of these Jesus traditions in Christian sermons or addresses, the earliest forms of the Gospels took shape. Three of our current Gospels then developed, in different localities and with distinct emphases, telling the story of Jesus in quite similar ways (Matthew, Mark, and Luke). Two of these (Matthew and Luke) contain a collection of Jesus' sayings and parables, again quite similar in the two Gospels, although ordered differently. The other Gospel (John) has a quite distinct layout, being organized around Jesus' trips to Jerusalem, apparently over three years, to participate in the great Jewish festivals that were observed in Jerusalem. This Gospel also has a distinctive content, style of writing, and theological outlook. Many interpreters hold that it contains some of the earliest and also some of the latest materials to be found in the four Gospels. It probably underwent several considerable expansions from its original form and content over several decades.

The material in the Gospels goes back to Jesus' actual words and deeds, but both underwent considerable expansion, it is believed, in the course of their use within the churches of different localities, reflecting changing social circumstances and theological perspectives in these localities. It is today very difficult to know with confidence just what parts of this Gospel tradition go back to Jesus himself. Many of the traditions come not from Jesus directly, but belong to the early decades of the Christian movement, when sayings of Jesus and stories about Jesus were being collected.

All four of the Gospels agree in considerable detail about the last days of Jesus in Jerusalem, about his death, and about the experiences of the disciples as the risen Jesus appeared to them. The Passion Narratives, beginning with Jesus' entry into

Jerusalem on Palm Sunday and concluding with the first Easter, may have been the first part of the Gospel story to have been set down in writing in detail. They became something like a Christian Passover narrative, providing for the church an equivalent narrative to that used at Passover by the Jewish community, relating the story of the Exodus and its conclusion when the firstborn sons of Egypt were slain and Israel was led by God from slavery into freedom.

The Formation of the Letters

The other basic part of the New Testament is the collection of letters from the apostle Paul and from the other apostles. To this one must add the book of Acts—a continuation of the Gospel of Luke that recounts the spread of Christianity throughout the Mediterranean world, concentrating especially on the journeys and experiences of Paul. One must also add the book of Revelation, a work akin to the book of Daniel in the Hebrew Bible, telling of the trials and testings that await the faithful Christian community at the end of history, before the consummation of all things as the risen Christ appears.

It seems likely that the letters of Paul were sent originally to particular congregations to help them address particular issues and questions facing them. These letters were shared with other congregations quite early, simply because of Paul's prestige and because of the value of the letters to the various congregations and their individual members. A major collection, perhaps introduced by the Letter to the Ephesians (written by a disciple of Paul if not by Paul himself), would have been in circulation toward the end of the first century c.e. And thus the New Testament in its two essential parts was available for copying and transmission throughout the entire Mediterranean world.

Apocryphal Christian Writings

Many Jewish writings were produced during the period from about 200 b.c.e. to 200 c.e., including the books of the Apocrypha mentioned above. Some of these writings had close similarities to the biblical books of Daniel and Revelation. They have come to be called "apocalyptic" works, writings that offer a revelation (the

71

word "apocalypse" means "revelation") of the end of the world, the fulfillment of God's purpose for Israel, and the destruction of evil. Marked by dreams and visions, by travels to heaven and to the underworld, by often bizarre imagery and strange symbolism, they are attributed to personalities from the Bible: Abraham, Moses, Job, Elijah, Baruch, Enoch, and many others. Among these writings are some that are "last words" or "testaments," presented as words addressed to the family or to the community by ancient biblical personalities such as Abraham, Moses, Job, the twelve sons of Jacob, and many others. Genesis 49, Deuteronomy 33, and II Samuel 23:1-7 are biblical "testaments," attributed respectively to Jacob, Moses, and David. These testaments sometimes also contain visions of the end of the world, but they are marked as well by wise counsel given by the dying patriarch to those being left behind. Such writings have been much studied in recent years and are currently available in new English translations.

It is less well known that the New Testament literature also continued to be produced long after the four Gospels, the book of Acts, the letters of Paul and the other apostles, and the book of Revelation had been accepted as the basic New Testament. The writings in the New Testament Apocrypha include other Gospels (of Peter, of Thomas, and of Philip, plus the Gnostic Gospel of Truth, for example), just as they include other revelations made to apostles other than John and many other letters attributed to the other apostles. Just as the Hebrew Bible did not come abruptly to an end, but was the product of discussions, debates, and eventual decisions as to which books belonged in the Hebrew Bible, so also the New Testament required the same kind of debates and discussion until a consensus was arrived at by the church councils of the early centuries.

The Canon

The canon of Hebrew Scriptures was fairly well established by about 100 C.E. No council of elders or authorities took a vote or adopted a formal decree as to the proper contents of the Hebrew Bible. The biblical writings accepted were those that had already been accepted by the community's use, for the most part. No question arose, of course, about the first five books of the Bible, the Torah. And few questions appeared with regard to the Former and Latter Prophets. Some debate took place regarding legal materials in the book of Ezekiel, but the issues were settled satisfactorily after additional rabbinical discussion and labor.

There were more debates regarding the proper contents of the Writings, the last and the most miscellaneous collection, but the Rabbis agreed that twelve Writings belonged (Psalms, Job, Proverbs, Ruth, Song of Songs, Ecclesiastes, Lamentations, Esther, Daniel, Ezra, Nehemiah, and Chronicles). The books of the Apocrypha, widely known and used in some Jewish circles, were rejected, in part because they were much in use within the growing Christian community, and in part because they were recognized to be later than the time of Ezra, who brought the definitive Torah back from Babylonia to Israel. Writings later than Ezra were considered to be suspect.

The many other writings found in the manuscripts that were not in the Apocrypha were also suspect, probably for the same reasons. Christian communities made a great deal of the apocalyptic works telling of the end of the world, and the Rabbis in time laid these aside, leaving them to the Christians. In addition, the Testaments and other Jewish works that were not apocalyptic, and that would seem to have been suitable for inclusion, were recognized to be later products, not a part of the ancient tradition, and were therefore not incorporated into the sacred writings.

As for the Christian community, the problem was more complex. The question of what belonged to the Hebrew Bible seemed less urgent for Christians than it was for the Jewish community. The Bible with the Apocrypha was accepted without question until the time of Jerome (late fourth and early fifth centuries c.e.). As Jerome completed his translation of the Hebrew Bible, he recognized that the Jewish canon was much shorter than that used by the Christian community, and he therefore called attention to this fact in his prefaces to the biblical books, suggesting a lesser authority for the apocryphal books. He also had much to do with the decision to leave out of the Christian Bible the other apocalyptic works, called by this time the

Pseudepigrapha (writings falsely assigned to the writers whose names they bore).

The contents of the New Testament were more fluid during the early Christian years. The Epistle to the Laodiceans, for example, was included (and is still included today) in some editions of Jerome's Latin translation of the Bible, the Vulgate. But the many later Gospels, Acts, Letters (Epistles), and Revelations were soon relegated to the noncanonical writings, or formally declared to be heretical. The many conflicts within the church during the first several centuries led finally to the adoption of lists of the writings that were canonical, those of lesser authority (deutero-canonical), and those with no authority at all.

Scripture and Jewish-Christian Relations

Evaluating Scripture's Significance

The question of Scripture is very important indeed for the relations of Jews and Christians. One issue, much neglected until recent times, is knowledge on the part of Christians of the place that the Mishnah and the Gemara (the Talmud) occupy in Jewish life and thought. Many Jewish scholars find the world of the Talmud more fascinating and challenging than that of the three-part Hebrew Bible itself, for the Talmud applies the Jewish Scripture to all facets and aspects of the common life, showing how Torah is to guide the people of God in ever-changing times and circumstances. And some Jews, as noted above, find the authority of Scripture to be broad and general, not literal at all.

For Christians too, of course, there are many different ways of understanding and defining the authority of Scripture. In some Protestant communities, the New Testament is so heavily stressed that the value and authority of the Old Testament and of the Apocrypha are very low indeed. Such communities deliberately define themselves as "New Testament" Christians.

Some Christians also have used the distinction between the Old and New Testaments to define the specific differences between the Jewish and the Christian communities today. In the Nazi period in Germany, some Christians came to view the Hebrew

Bible with hostility. Many others interpreted the distinction between law and grace so sharply that the Hebrew Bible came to be viewed as law and the New Testament as grace, thus making the Christian "Old Testament" valuable for Christians primarily in showing what the Christian did *not* believe. These issues were reviewed in chapters 1 and 2.

Today, the Hebrew Bible and the New Testament stand together, usually with the Apocrypha, as one single collection of sacred writings for the Christian community, with the later apocalyptic writings also of great value for the study of the Bible and of Judaism and Christianity. In addition, some Christian scholars (but not yet a sufficient number) are seriously at work on the Mishnah and the Gemara, learning (with the aid of Jewish teachers) the contents and the best modes of investigation of this large body of Jewish literature and lore.

How Jewish Is the New Testament?

The New Testament, though written in Hellenistic Greek, is a thoroughly Jewish document. Greek was widely known and used in the Jewish world, in Palestine as well as in other parts of the eastern Mediterranean world. The Greek of the "Old Testament" Apocrypha and of the New Testament has a strong Hebrew/Aramaic coloring, as is to be expected, since much of it is literature either translated from Hebrew or Aramaic or formed by Semitic-speaking writers. It is a mistake, therefore, to consider the New Testament to belong to an entirely different world than that of the Hebrew Bible or of the Mishnah. The New Testament reflects Jewish tradition throughout.

Scholars have long recognized that both the Mishnah and the New Testament contain and reflect traditional teachings, modes of interpretation, and ways of viewing the world. Such Jewish tradition is therefore an additional source, beyond the Hebrew Bible and the Apocrypha, for both the New Testament and the Mishnah. Some of this traditional teaching has been discovered in the Dead Sea Scrolls and in other recently located Jewish documents, but of course much of it has to be inferred from the New Testament and from the Mishnah. The important point is to recognize how Jewish the New Testament is. This caution is particularly in order for those Christian groups that identify the New Testament as of unique authority—groups that may, as a consequence, tend to separate the New Testament too sharply from its Jewish setting and world. The result has sometimes been to compare all other Jewish writings unfavorably with the authoritative New Testament. Christians, of course, may be expected to find definitive teachings and disclosures in the New Testament. But it is inappropriate for them to use their own document as the norm for judging the literary, historical, ethical, and religious qualities of the Mishnah and the Gemara, for example.

Recent Translations of the Bible and Jewish/Christian Relations

The many new translations of the Hebrew Bible, the Apocrypha, and the New Testament, often done collaboratively by Jewish and Christian scholars, have done much to bring the Jewish and the Christian communities together in the study of the biblical materials. And the strong emphasis in recent years on a variety of approaches to biblical study (historical, literary, sociological, history-of-religions) has also helped make the study of the Bible a positive contribution to Jewish/Christian relations rather than a hindrance and a burden to good relations. May that happy development continue and grow!

Suggested Readings

Barth, M. *Israel and the Church.*
Buber, M. *The Prophetic Faith.*
————. *Two Types of Faith.*
Küng, H., and W. Kasper. *Christians and Jews.*
Petuchowski, J., and M. Brocke. *The Lord's Prayer and Jewish Liturgy.*
Plaut, W. G. *The Torah: A Modern Commentary.*
Sandmel, S. *A Jewish Understanding of the New Testament.*
————. *Anti-Semitism in the New Testament.*
————. *The Hebrew Scriptures.*
Steinsaltz, A. *The Essential Talmud.*
Tanenbaum, M. *Evangelicals and Jews in Conversation.*
Yadin, Y. *The Temple Scroll.*

CHAPTER FOUR

UNDERSTANDING OUR GOD CONCEPTS

A Jewish Outlook

Jews and Christians are on common ground as monotheists. Certainly we differ in our definitions of God and in the ways in which we relate to God. We begin, however, with the same understanding of the nature of God and of God's unity.

In seeking to formulate definitions of God, Jews and Christians can begin together with the first words of the first chapter of the book of Genesis: "In the beginning, God. . . ." This affirmation of a God unlimited by time or space is beautifully expressed in the "Yigdal," a hymn found in many Jewish and Christian prayer books. In the first verse we sing:

> We praise the living God,
> For ever praise His name,
> Who was and is and is to be
> For e'er the same;
> The One eternal God
> Before our world appears,
> And there can be no end of time
> Beyond His years.
> *(Gates of Prayer,* pp. 732-33)

From this belief in God's existence prior to the calling into existence of the heavens and the earth, we move on to the development of our understanding of God as creator of both a planned, orderly natural universe and a pattern for life on this

79

earth. This understanding did not arise full-blown, but developed over a considerable period of time, in the midst of several other ways of viewing creation.

Two Accounts of Creation

In the Babylonian creation story called Enuma Elish, one of the most famous creation stories of the ancient Near East, the high gods chose as their champion to defend themselves against Tiamat, who had turned against the other gods, the powerful war-god Marduk, the deity of the Babylonian empire. Marduk, after having won the battle in heaven, created the universe out of the body of the slain Tiamat. He then fashioned humankind to serve the gods, using some of the blood of the slain Kingu, the champion appointed by Tiamat.

Enuma Elish shows how the creation of the universe arose out of the conflict in the heavens among the gods. The creation of human beings was not the goal of the entire creative process but was almost an afterthought. The heavenly world was to be served by the earthly, thus relieving the deities of some of their onerous tasks. Other texts from Babylonia also show that the development of human life on the planet depended on the intervention of friendly deities to prevent the hostile gods from doing harm or violence to earthly beings. The great Babylonian flood hero, Utnapishtim, was saved along with his family, only because the deity Ea whispered the news that the flood was coming and told Utnapishtim to prepare the ark and save himself and his family, keeping all others unaware of the flood to come.

The creation story with which Hebrew Scriptures opens is strikingly different. In the first place, there is a single Beginner, out of whose "voice" each facet of the universe is created in five days. Some theologians think of the "voice" as logos or instrument. No matter what the terminology, and no matter whether one is a creationist or an evolutionist, here we find not only a single Beginner, but a consistent, orderly pattern of bringing the universe into existence.

Human beings are created on the sixth day, not to serve the deity (as in the Babylonian story), but to care for God's creation.

Created in the image of God, mortals are appointed to exercise authority, under God's overarching sovereignty, over all that God has created.

The story in chapter 2 of Genesis, which again tells of the creation of the first human pair, also tells of God's placing them in the garden of Eden, stressing that the couple is to care for the garden and is to live in companionship with each other and with God. Such a robust humanism in the portrayal of the purpose of the creation of the universe has no parallel in any of the other creation stories of the ancient world.

The other tremendously important factor that is unique in the creation story, as we find it in Hebrew Scriptures, is that at the end of every step of the creative process there is a statement that God saw what He had made, and it was good. Such a view was not common in the ancient world. Life was cruel, an arena of perpetual struggle and warfare, of famine and blight. Knowing this, the biblical writers stressed the goodness of God's work in creation. Though sin appears in the garden with the first human pair, the goodness of creation is not obliterated by sin. However, the sins of human beings bring great grief to God. After Adam and Eve have been driven from the garden, their son Cain slays his brother Abel and becomes a fugitive and wanderer on earth. Then human sin leads to the terrible flood. But at each of these stages in human failing, God demonstrates grace along with judgment. Adam and Eve leave the garden and go out to people the earth and to care for it, clothed in animal skins. Cain wanders throughout the earth, but with a mark upon him that prevents his being slain. And the vast flood, while threatening to undo the whole of God's creation, actually serves to cleanse it, to preserve each species of life and to provide a fresh start, and most importantly, to establish the basis for covenantal relationships between God and humankind.

God's Relationship to Humankind

God's Salvation in History

Most ancient peoples have their myths, their stories of the lives of their gods, focused on the heavens or on the earth-times that lie well behind and beyond human history. Hebrew Scriptures' myths, however, are in the form of ancestral narratives, stories about the patriarchs and matriarchs of the people. Here, in these narratives, the concerns of God are with this earth and its peoples. By the same token, these stories enable us to see the ways in which our ancestors developed a deeper and broader understanding of God and their covenantal relationship with God. God does not change in the process, but the concept of God changes.

Abraham is considered the first Jew, because he was the first human being who conceived of one God of a tribe or family, an unseen Deity who controlled the various forces of nature which many peoples worshiped as separate sources of the powers that influenced their lives. The covenant that God makes with Abraham is that he will be the father of a great people, that he will dwell in a fertile land bestowed by God, and that God will be with him, providing guidance and protection. In return, Abraham is commanded to be a blessing, to be one through whom God's blessing will be extended to all the peoples of the earth (Genesis 12:2-3).

Jacob gives us still another understanding of God in terms of a personal relationship. It was Jacob who wrestled with the angel, wrestled with his conscience, wrestled with God within. Jacob felt that God would forgive him and allow him to grow in acceptance of responsibility both to God and to his fellow human beings. In Jacob's change from a grasping, selfish person to one capable of repenting and responding to God within, we sense a new and profound commitment to a personal God. As Jacob (the name meaning "the supplanter") became Israel (meaning "the upright one of God"), God accepted the repentant sinner into a covenant in which God again promised that the descendants of Abraham and of Jacob would occupy God's special territory, where they would be fruitful and multiply (Genesis 35:9-13).

The God of History

Moving on to the book of Exodus, with Moses we come to know a liberating God who leads an enslaved people out of bondage. At the foot of Mount Sinai these emancipated Hebrews are joined by the Midianites, led by Jethro, Moses' father-in-law, and perhaps by tribes from "the other side of the river" (the "Ivri"). Together they seek God's guidance and support in their efforts to settle in the Fertile Crescent, which these people believe is God's special territory, the same that God had promised to the patriarchs. God agrees to enter into this covenant with this new coalition of peoples, if they will accept God's Ten Commandments as the moral law by which they will live in harmonious relationship with God and according to God's ethical pattern with their fellow human beings. When the people accept the responsibility to live according to God's moral law by affirming "we will willingly do it" (Deuteronomy 5:24 JPS), they are almost ready to begin the torturous forty-year journey through the wilderness to the promised land.

Only one more important lesson remains to be taught before the wilderness wandering begins. Not only must the people be loyal to the one God with whom they have entered into covenant, they must know how to respond to God. This is delineated very explicitly for them in the passage known in Jewish liturgy as the "Sh'ma":

> Hear, O Israel! The LORD is our God, the LORD alone. You shall love the LORD your God with all your heart and with all your soul and with all your might. Take to heart these instructions with which I charge you this day. Impress them upon your children. Recite them when you stay at home and when you are away, when you lie down and when you get up. Bind them as a sign on your hand and let them serve as a symbol on your forehead; inscribe them on the doorposts of your house and on your gates. (Deuteronomy 6:4-9 JPS)

From that awesome moment at Sinai to this present day, the primary command in Jewish life has been to accept the concept that God is one, and to relate to God by loving God with our minds, our hearts, our deeds.

The other important lesson to be learned here about this liberating God was that God was not confined at Sinai but could be with the people in their long journey and would enter into the promised land with them to guide and protect them, so long as they kept their part of the covenant bond.

The Universal God

It is important to note here that, even before the covenants with the patriarchs, God had entered into a covenant with humankind. At the end of the Flood story, in the ninth chapter of Genesis, God promises that never again will God cause a flood to destroy all living beings. That covenant is sealed by the appearance of a rainbow in the sky. Moreover, in the early chapters of Genesis, God provides seven Noahide laws, which are the first ethical commandments to serve as guidelines for basic relationships with God and between human beings. This is an early emphasis in Jewish teaching on one universal God and one humanity.

Universalism reaches its climax in the Jews' relationship with God through the witness of the prophets. At the same time, we must also recognize that many of the teachings of the prophets underscored a particularism in the relationship of God to this "chosen people." Amos, for example, proclaims that God has the power to punish all peoples for their transgressions, even though Israel is singled out for the most dire consequences of their sins because "you alone have I singled out of all the families of the earth" (Amos 3:2 JPS).

Jeremiah, too, includes in his teachings both the conviction that God has a special relationship with Israel and the realization that the God of Israel is also the God of all peoples. Jeremiah's recognition of the unique bond between God and Israel reaches a climax in his prophecy:

> See, a time is coming—declares the LORD—when I will make a new covenant with the House of Israel and the House of Judah. It will not be like the covenant I made with their fathers, when I took them by the hand to lead them out of the land of Egypt, a covenant which they broke, so that I rejected them—declares the LORD. But such is the covenant I will make with the House of Israel after these days—declares the LORD: I will put My Teaching into their inmost being and inscribe it upon their hearts. Then I will be their God, and they shall be My people. (Jeremiah 31:31-33 JPS)

God in Post-Biblical Jewish Literature

The Jews' quest for God does not stop with Hebrew Scriptures. In both the Talmud and the Midrash the Rabbis continue to explore both the particularism of the covenant between God and Israel, and the universalism of God's love and caring for all humankind. Nowhere, though, do we find the Jewish understanding of God more clearly or more succinctly defined than in the Thirteen Principles of Faith, enunciated by Moses ben Maimon, also known as Maimonides, a renowned twelfth-century interpreter of Scripture and of rabbinic law. The Principles are still included in every orthodox prayer book. Here are those Principles from Maimonides' creed that are his summary definition of God:

> I believe with perfect faith that the Creator, blessed be His Name, is the Author and Guide of everything that has been created, and that He alone has made, does make, and will make all things.
> I believe with perfect faith that the Creator, blessed be His Name, is a unity, and that there is no unity in any manner like unto His, our God Who was, is, and will be.
> I believe with perfect faith that the Creator, blessed be His Name, is not a body, that He is free of all the accidents of matter, that He is not any form whatsoever.
> I believe with perfect faith that the Creator, blessed be His Name, is the first and the last, that there was no being prior to the Creator and there will be no being that will follow Him.
> I believe with perfect faith that to the Creator, blessed be His Name, and to Him alone it is right to pray. It is not right to pray to any being beside Him.
> I believe with perfect faith that the Creator, blessed be His Name, knows every deed of the children of man and all their thoughts. As it is said, it is He that fashioneth the hearts of them all, that giveth heed to all their deeds.
> I believe with perfect faith that the Creator, blessed be His Name, rewards those that keep His commandments and punishes those that transgress them.

The Personal God

One more aspect of the Jewish understanding of God remains to be explored. In Judaism there is a primary emphasis on the relationship of God to the community, because the Torah was given not to an individual but to the community of Israel. It is also the total community that is responsible for maintaining the covenant bond with God. At the same time there did develop, especially with Psalms and the book of Job, continuing with the Sayings of the Fathers in the Mishnah, and on into medieval and contemporary Jewish philosophy, a definite commitment to a personal God.

This reaches a climax in twentieth-century Jewish thought with the writings of Martin Buber, and especially with his I-Thou relationship. There is no way to explain simply the I-Thou concept in Buber's writings. It is a spiritual bond that can be felt and experienced rather than verbalized. Buber does, however, offer us one summary of this special understanding of relationship, when he writes in *I and Thou*:

> The primary word *I-Thou* can be spoken only with the whole being. Concentration and fusion into the whole being can never take place through my agency, nor can it ever take place without me. I become through my relation to the *Thou;* as I become *I,* I say *Thou.*
> All real living is meeting.

The God of Jews and Christians

One final question we must ask ourselves: Do Jews and Christians worship the same God? My answer, from a Jewish perspective, is *yes!* We worship the same God, though a God somewhat differently defined, to Whom we relate in different ways, and to Whom we come out of a variety of experiences. Nevertheless, this is the same God Who is Creator of us all and Who is potentially in contact with every human being.

Our definition of God is also conditioned by the environment in which the individual and the community seek God. In Judaism the great emphasis from earliest times has been on the Unity of God, the Oneness. Why is this? Because Jews, in the pagan world that surrounded them, were constantly confronted with beliefs in many gods. The Prophets insistently warned the people against pursuing these various gods for ulterior purposes: added protection for themselves and their crops in lands thought to have been previously dominated by one or another pagan deity. Similar warnings and admonitions by rabbis and sages over the centuries have caused the emphasis in Judaism to be on the retention of an absolute Unity. No matter how we are conditioned, though, or how differently we define God, we Jews and Christians shall continue to seek a more deeply spiritual relationship with our God. We must also continue together to find ways to respond to the challenge of the prophet Malachi: "Have we not all one father? Did not one God create us? Why do we break faith with one another, profaning the covenant of our fathers?" (Malachi 2:10 JPS).

UNDERSTANDING OUR GOD CONCEPTS

A Christian Outlook

We have set for ourselves the massive task of sketching in broad outline what Jews and Christians believe about God. It is necessary to make clear that not only is there no unanimity on this question; many Jews and Christians prefer not to address the question at all. We do better, they think, if we talk about the issues that confront us in this world, not about such speculative matters as come up when we talk theology. Judaism, it is sometimes said, is a way of life, not a religious system that requires a theology. Theology is a Christian discipline, one that Judaism can do without.

The fact is, however, that theological matters are of enormous importance to Jewish/Christian relations; if we lay such matters aside we only defer the problems that they will surely cause in time. One need only mention the Christian doctrine of the Trinity to see that theological issues cannot be bracketed out of discussions aimed at deepening understanding between Jews and Christians.

Rabbi Falk has already discussed our common understandings of the nature of God as Creator. He has reviewed the process through which the ancient Israelites developed and affirmed a faith in one God, beginning with Abraham's tribal deity and ultimately coming to affirm a universal deity through the teachings of the great prophets. Our next task is to deal more directly with Jewish and Christian understandings of how God relates to human beings, and how the search for fundamental meaning in human life has produced critical issues on which Jews and Christians have often been divided.

God in Relation to Human Beings

God as Just and Merciful

Saving history is marked by God's judgment and God's mercy. Over and again God comes to hold the people to account, making clear, as Israel's leaders make clear, that God's judgment must fall upon the faithless community. But the saving God is still active in judgment. The judgment is itself a sign that God will not leave Israel alone, will not merely abandon a faithless people. Rather, *because* God is faithful, God comes in wrath and judgment, for that is what Israel's conduct calls for. But judgment is not all. God also finds a way to be merciful. One element of God's mercy is God's suffering with Israel in the punishment, in the judgment. God administers judgment and also feels the weight of the judgment as it falls (Hosea 11). Another dimension of mercy shows up in the way in which God relents of planned judgment and comes as Savior of a faithless people. God's mercy outstrips the divine wrath. Judgment continues for three or more generations, but God's mercy is extended to the thousandth generation (the apparent meaning of Exodus 20:5-6 and 34:6-7). In fact, the very character and nature of God are best described as "merciful" (Exodus 34:6; Hosea 11:7-9; Jeremiah 3:12).

The entire biblical story of God's judgment and mercy displays this priority of divine mercy over judgment. While Israel is held strictly to account when it fails the God of the covenant, and while God's Torah (teaching, guidance, law) is there to enable Israel to know the way in which to walk, Israel's failings are addressed by a patient parent, a loving Father, a devoted and fiercely caring Mother, always intent upon finding a way to place Israel on the path of faithfulness.

God of the Oppressed

The historical community of Israel begins in Egypt, formed from a band of oppressed slaves of the Pharaoh there who cry out to God in pain. No terms for God are more important than those that speak of God's partiality for the poor, the hungry, the oppressed, the suffering of the earth. God hears the cry of the people in pain and misery, and God raises up leaders among the people to respond to the injustices that have produced such pain and misery. Here lies the revolutionary power of biblical religion. God demands that the oppression of peoples come to an end, for that is not in the long run endurable to God, and should not be to God's people.

Interventions by God to save the oppressed may be miraculous and unrelated to human deeds, but they regularly are the product of God's raising up historical leaders to come to the rescue of the oppressed. Exodus 3 provides the pattern: The outcry of the suffering reaches God; God determines to act to bring justice; and God singles out a human agent to be the instrument of divine deliverance. It is the task of Israel's religious leaders to sensitize and attune the conscience of the people so that they will recognize God's primary and fundamental concern for the oppressed of earth. Nothing in the Hebrew Bible is more characteristic of the God of Israel than this bias in favor of the oppressed.

God Hidden and Revealed

The Hebrew Bible speaks much about God, assumes God's active presence in their world, and offers praise and petitions to God regularly. In many respects, the community that is portrayed in the Hebrew Bible is deeply religious, with its life surrounded and regulated by the religious requirements developed over the centuries. At the same time, this community is very reluctant to say too much about the inner nature and character of God. Such reticence is evident in the name borne by God, the personal name, probably pronounced "Yahweh" or "Yahaweh." This name, unlike most names in the Hebrew language, is not given any etymological meaning, although it is clear from Exodus 3:14 that the name is taken to be related to the verb "to be," "to come to be," or "to cause to be." The expression in Exodus, however, seems designed to withhold information rather than to give it. The name "YHWH" has vowels belonging to another word and is to be pronounced "Adonay" ("The

Lord"). The inner character of the deity will be discerned, if at all, through God's *deeds,* through the way in which the deity sees to the life of Israel in the world.

Rarely is it claimed that any prophet or leader or worshiper actually sees God. Moses is reminded, when he asks to see God's glory, that he cannot see the face of God; he may see only God's back as the deity passes by atop the holy mountain (Exodus 33:17-23). Isaiah sees the Lord in the Temple (Isaiah 6), but the description given reveals only the swirling clouds that comprise God's train, and the surrounding seraphim. Job cries out bitterly to see the God who has abandoned him, or so he believes, confident that if only he could confront God directly he would be able successfully to plead his case (Job 19:23-27). Psalmists plead with God to come to their aid, and frequently they acknowledge that God does so. But we do not get descriptions of the deity who comes to bring healing, help, and salvation.

But this invisible God is the most real of all realities to prophets and psalmists and sages. God's mark is left upon the creation itself, for Wisdom was present with God at the creation, rejoicing and singing God's praises (Proverbs 8). History displays God's workings, though these deeds of God are often strange and mysterious to human sight (Isaiah 28:21). And even when God seems disposed no longer to come to the aid of the people, the faithful know nothing better to do than to continue to plead with God to do so (Psalm 44, for example).

Israel's prophets go to great lengths to protect the divine integrity. They remind the people that there are *no indispensable means to divine revelation,* none at all. The Temple of Solomon was revered greatly even by the great prophets, but the Temple was not essential to God's revelation (Jeremiah 7). Nor was the ark of the covenant: a day would come when its loss would be of no consequence at all (Jeremiah 3:16). The holy city Zion could be threatened with complete destruction (Micah 3:12), and the very people of the covenant could be replaced (Amos 9:7). Nothing in the entire creation is an indispensable representation of God or an indispensable instrument in the fulfillment of God's purposes for the creation.

God of the Future

Even so, Israel was encouraged always to keep its eye upon the future, upon *God's* future. The promises made to Israel's ancestors are sure of realization, but in God's own way. Many images appear in the Bible showing the time of consummation of God's work on earth. Some images stress the social and political dimensions, when God will raise up the right kind of descendant of King David who will exercise just rule from Jerusalem over all God's earth (Isaiah 9:1-7). Some point to a time of peace and righteousness, when nations settle their disputes peacefully and warfare comes to an end (Isaiah 2:2-4; Micah 4:1-4). Others speak of internal changes in the very depths of the heart, so that God's demands are kept spontaneously and naturally as the hearts of people are set right (Jeremiah 31:31-34). Still other texts portray a world, a universe, that has been transformed by God's action, nothing less than "new heavens and a new earth" (Isaiah 65:17; 66:22 RSV).

This portrayal of God as the sovereign of the future is of incalculable importance for Israelite religion. God is creator, just judge, lawgiver, sovereign of the historical process, one who suffers with the suffering, who supports the poor and the oppressed. God is also the One who sees finally to the needs of earth, who will not let human beings finally destroy all that has been created and sustained. The promises for the future do not, of course, *guarantee* a future for the universe. But they do clearly affirm the confidence of the people of Israel that God has not abandoned the world. God is seeing to earth's needs, to human need, bringing all to wholeness in a time that lies ahead.

Confidence in the future also gives impetus to the community to seek *now* to realize what lies ahead in God's purpose. The visions of the Consummation are a challenge and a lure, a drawing power that continually beckons the community to realize *now* as much of that coming and sure fulfillment as is possible.

Problems in Our Understandings of God

Where do the problems lie in Jewish and Christian understandings of God? As noted above, theological discussions are not the pressure points for many persons. Even so, the ways we speak about God are important, and have been divisive, in Jewish-Christian relations. A few of the most important differences need to be discussed. Some of these are almost inseparable from our discussion of Jesus (the subject of the next chapter) and will be dealt with here as well as briefly mentioned there.

God the Savior from Sin

As we pointed out above, the Hebrew Bible stresses God's saving and redeeming activity in history and promises the fulfillment of the divine purposes in a Day of Consummation that lies ahead. God as Savior is not only the Savior from the sin of the people and the individual but also the Savior in all times of historical danger and difficulty—in this concrete world of which we are a part today. The Christian community, following the lead of the New Testament, has stressed through the ages that God intervenes in the lives of individuals and groups to break the hold of sin upon the world, bringing liberation from sin that leads to death. God is thus the Savior from that spiritual power of sin that enslaves and threatens to undo every individual the world over, and throughout all history. In Jesus Christ, God has entered our historical world with such decisiveness and authority that the power of sin and death over individuals, groups, and institutions is definitively broken. It is not that sin no longer touches those delivered by God through Christ; the claim is made—a bold claim indeed—that those who give allegiance to Jesus as the Christ by the power of the Spirit are now able to overcome the power of sin and death through this gift of divine grace and love. They claim a gift extended to all persons and groups, and in the life of the Christian community they live mutually affirming this great gift of love and supporting one another in reclaiming the gift daily as they live out their lives. Thus, salvation is at one and the same time God's saving power present in the community and the world to enable the faithful to affirm and embody God's transforming of a world where injustice and cruelty and mean-spiritedness are widespread, and also God's definitive act through Christ to break the hold of that cosmic power present in all cultures, all groups, all institutions, all individuals—the reality called sin.

When one reads the New Testament, one sees how central this

notion of salvation from sin really is. It is one of the dominant elements of Paul's message, especially as seen in the Letter to the Romans. Sin and death hold the world in thralldom, but in fact God's action in Jesus Christ is such that sin and death no longer really have sway in the transformed world. It is the responsibility of the Christian community to declare this new freedom from sin and death and invite all persons to share in it.

In the Jewish community through the ages, the picture of salvation found in the Hebrew Scriptures has been adopted and elaborated in such a way as to give much less emphasis to this notion of sin and death as powers that possess the whole of human history, displayed in the life of both institutions and individuals. Judaism has always stressed the point that the Jewish community has been charged to observe God's Torah, God's concrete guidance for life in this world. Judaism has also stressed the point that the community and its individual members *can* keep the Torah. Sin is an immense and mysterious power in the world, indeed. But God provides the way to fulfill the divine covenant, to hold fast to the path of faithfulness. God's world is still a good world, though terribly distorted and bent by human misdeeds and failings. The claim upon God's people is to *be* the people God has called them to be—a recognizable entity in the world, keeping covenant and faith and displaying God's continuing love for a people that fail in their covenant obligations.

This difference in outlook about God and God's salvation will be discussed further when we speak of election, covenant, and mission. There is no doubt that the difference is there, and it should not be covered up. I remember vividly a comment by a dear friend who had a family background in both Judaism and Christianity. He said, "It seems to me that Judaism is a religion to guide one's life *in* this world, while Christianity is a religion to liberate one *from* life in this world." There is no doubt that Christianity has often stressed salvation from a sinful world and stressed much too little the Christian affirmation that salvation is *for* life in this world, as well as preparation for eternal life with God.

The Trinity

Jewish/Christian discussions and debates often focus upon the Christian understanding of the Trinity and of Jesus Christ as the Son of God. The radical monotheism (the term is from H. Richard Niebuhr, a Christian theologian who strongly commended this monotheistic faith) of Judaism and of the Hebrew Scriptures is frequently contrasted with the trinitarianism of the Christian community. The contrast is real and is not to be minimized. It is, however, a misunderstanding of Christianity to consider that trinitarian belief in fact means the worship of three deities. It is true, of course, that through the centuries the church has sometimes so strongly stressed the divinity of Jesus that Jesus has appeared to be a second God, and the chief God indeed, alongside of God the Creator.

This development is accompanied by another: the Spirit may also be stressed so strongly by charismatic groups that the Spirit, the "third person of the Trinity," looms more significant than God the Creator or Jesus Christ as the Word made flesh. Thus, it is clearly possible for the church to overemphasize one of the "persons" of the Trinity so much that the intention of the doctrine of the Trinity is obscured.

What *is* that intention? It is precisely to affirm the *unity*, the oneness of God in the face of such overemphasis upon Jesus as the Christ and the saving Word or upon the Holy Spirit as the enlivening and sustaining presence in the continuing life of the Christian community. The doctrine of the Trinity, present in the Bible according to much Christian belief but clearly not developed there as a Christian doctrine, seeks to be faithful to the actual experience of the Christian community and its individual members, which experience includes the experience of God the Creator and Sustainer of all life continuing to be just the Creator and Sustainer that the Hebrew Bible affirms and that Jesus affirms God to be.

The community and its members also experience Jesus as God's Messiah, the anointed one sent by God to bring consummation of the divine purpose on earth, freeing God's people and summoning them to declare and to work for the consummation that has now begun in Christ. This Christ is God's

95

Word and God's Wisdom, the one present with God the Creator from the very creation itself, and indeed active with God the Creator in the creation. More and more, what the Christian community knew to say about God, it tended to say also about Jesus as the Christ. Jesus was experienced as the son of Mary and Joseph, fully human and fully a part of historical existence. But Jesus was also experienced as the eternal Word and Wisdom of God, now fully enfleshed (incarnated) as Jesus of Nazareth, son of Mary and Joseph.

The Christian community experienced Jesus as at once the historical Jesus of Nazareth who suffered and died on a Roman cross, was buried, and clearly belonged to the realm of the dead, and also as raised from death by God, inaugurating the New Age when death can no longer claim forever those who die. With Jesus' death and ascension to the place of honor reserved for him at God's right hand, the age of the Holy Spirit is inaugurated. This same Jesus, who was the Word and Wisdom of God and who was taken up to share in the glory reserved for all destined to join him before God, is now present in the church in the Spirit, actively present in the church as the very Body of Christ.

The point is that the early Christian community, and the church through the centuries, has sought by means of the doctrine of the Trinity to affirm its actual experience of one God present in the church and the world as the Holy Trinity. The church came to speak, not of one God present in different modes of being, but of one substance in three persons, using distinctions that had proved useful in philosophical discussions of Christian faith. Perhaps the clearer way to speak of the Trinity today is to say that the one God is actively present in the experience of Christian believers as (1) Creator and Sustainer, the One to whom we owe our very being; (2) Word and Wisdom, imparting truth and condescending love to the whole world and definitively breaking the power of sin and death to give liberation to all; and (3) illuminating, inspiring, and guiding divine spiritual presence that presents to the community of faith and its individual members both the Creator/Sustainer and the Word/Wisdom/ transforming love that is the Christ. Thus, the full presence of the one God is a trinitarian presence, a presence that our forebears have known and witnessed to, a presence in the life and worship of the church, and a presence in the totality of the universe. Christianity, like Judaism, affirms a monotheistic faith. But Christianity, unlike Judaism, speaks of that faith and witnesses to it in trinitarian terms.

Law and Grace

Christianity often has spoken of God under two aspects and has associated the two aspects of God with the "Old" and the "New" Testaments. The "Old" Testament God is a God demanding stern justice and faithfulness, while the "New" Testament God is a God (known in Jesus Christ) of love and forgiveness. We spoke of this caricature in our discussion of the Scriptures (chapter 2); here it is only necessary to remind readers of the mischief that this caricature continues to do in Jewish-Christian relations. Monotheistic faith, clearly, will have nothing to do with such a notion, but it persists as Christians are all too prone to speak of the *view* of God to be found in the Hebrew Bible and in Judaism as of a deity whose fundamental characteristic is stern and implacable demand for faithfulness to the divine law, while the *true* picture of God, found in the New Testament, is of a deity who accepts the sinner while a sinner and displays an extraordinary readiness—because of Jesus' sacrificial death—to forgive sinners.

It cannot be stressed too strongly that law and grace go together, in the Hebrew Bible and in Judaism as well as in the New Testament and in Christianity. The gift of the divine law is itself a gift of grace; the demands of the law are the demands of a holy God. Jesus affirmed this as strongly as anyone, and Paul affirmed it as well. The demands of God can be *presented* and *understood* in narrow-minded and legalistic ways, and they have been within the Jewish community and within the Christian community from time to time and in various localities. But law and grace equally characterize the reality of God's dealings with the people of God and with the world; they should never be played off against each other.

We can see, then, that Jewish and Christian doctrines of God are very close to each other. Ancient distinctions sometimes went so far as to display the God of the "Old" Testament as a demonic power to be discarded entirely by the Christian community (in the thought of the heretic Marcion and even more strongly in the teaching of the Manichaeans). And even today, Christians, and the public at large, carelessly speak of an "Old Testament" God of wrath whom surely the contemporary world has outgrown and discarded. The harm done to Jewish-Christian relations by such misstatements and caricatures continues to be very considerable. It is long past time for such notions to be discarded as wrong.

Suggested Readings

Baeck, L. *Judaism and Christianity.*

Klenicki, L., and G. Wigoder. *A Dictionary of the Jewish-Christian Dialogue.*

Oesterreicher, J. *Brothers in Hope,* vol. 5, essay: "Deicide as a Theological Problem."

Van Buren, P. A Theology of the Jewish-Christian Reality: Part II—*A Christian Theology of the People Israel.*

CHAPTER FIVE

UNDERSTANDING OUR RELATIONSHIP TO JESUS

A Jewish Outlook

M any years ago the Central Conference of American Rabbis held its annual convention in Estes Park, Colorado. A number of the Rabbis from the East reserved two Pullman cars for the long journey from New York. It was a delightful trip, enhanced greatly by the diligent, courteous porter who attended to their every need. At the end of the journey, the porter brushed each man's suit once again, and then as the train stopped at the station, he descended to the platform to assist the Rabbis as they stepped off the train, and hopefully to receive tangible expressions of their appreciation.

The first Rabbi descended the steps, shook hands with the porter, and complimented him on the service he had rendered. But not a single dollar bill! The second man followed, expressed his thanks profusely, but nothing more. This same routine continued until the last man was about to depart. By this time the porter was beside himself. Two days and two nights with this group, but no tip had been forthcoming! Finally, as the last Rabbi shook hands with John, he too expressed his appreciation, and then added that the men had taken up a collection to show the porter their gratitude for his fine service. He presented John with five hundred dollars from the entire group.

The porter almost fainted with relief. He pulled himself together, though, and responded graciously to his benefactor. John said: "You Rabbis are certainly fine gentlemen, and I appreciate your gift. I always knew you Jews couldn't have killed our Lord. You must have just worried him to death." Perhaps there is more wisdom in the porter's statement than we realize at first glance.

Unlike some of our Christian contemporaries, most Jews do not find it a problem to understand Jesus, the man. The historicity of Jesus does not present great problems to us because we are accustomed in Hebrew Scriptures to rely on secondary sources for much of our historical background. If we were looking only for primary sources as the basis on which to understand our patriarchs, or even Moses, our greatest prophet, it would be extremely difficult to develop a historical perspective. Fortunately, there are secondary sources, some of which come out of an oral tradition, some of which come possibly from earlier primary sources that we cannot identify. In any case they give us an ability to piece together a story that provides a foundation upon which we can establish an understanding of the great leaders and teachers in our tradition. The same is true with Jesus. Unfortunately, the only significant primary sources for the period in which Jesus lived and taught make very little if any mention of him, so we rely on secondary sources, like the Gospels, for our basic historic outline. Many scholars believe that the Synoptic Gospels are based, in part at least, on an earlier historic source that, for the want of a better name, we call the "Q" document ("Q" stands for *Quelle,* meaning source). We do not know much about that source, but the secondary sources of the Synoptics and of John give us a foundation on which to understand Jesus, his life and his teachings.

Jesus the Jew

We know, of course, that Jesus was a Jew. He was born a Jew, and he was raised as a Jew in Galilee, one of the most beautiful, fertile areas of Palestine. Jesus studied as a Jew, and there are scholars who believe that when we read in the Gospels that, at the age of twelve, Jesus spoke before the elders in the synagogue, this may have been an occasion comparable to our Bar Mitzvah. We are not certain that the Bar Mitzvah tradition goes back that far, but it may. And it certainly would not be unusual that he was becoming Bar Mitzvah at the age of twelve, instead of the traditional age today of thirteen, because young men matured even earlier in those days than do adolescents today. For his rite of passage into Jewish religious adulthood, Jesus would have read from the Torah and then would have given an explanation of what he had read and what it had meant to him in terms of his relationship to Judaism.

So Jesus studied as a Jew, and later he taught as a Jew. All that Jesus taught was based either on Hebrew Scriptures or on the oral Law as found collected in the Mishnah and later in the great anthology called the Talmud. He was acquainted with both the written tradition and the oral tradition, and there is nothing that is quoted from Jesus in the New Testament that does not find its source in either Hebrew Scriptures or in the Talmud. Jesus, to the best of our knowledge, lived his brief life in Judea and had very limited contact with the gentile world. He was a teacher of Jews, a rabbi. *Rabbi*, as you know, is a Hebrew word that means teacher, and Jesus is referred to in the New Testament as rabbi. He probably followed in the rabbinic tradition of Hillel, a liberal interpreter of the Law and of the tradition, who lived a generation before Jesus.

And Jesus died as a Jew. When Christian Sunday school classes come to visit the Temple, we explain how we worship and study in our sanctuary and in our religious school, and then we ask for questions. Eventually one bright youngster will ask about Jesus since we haven't mentioned Jesus in the discussion. I will respond that Jesus was born a Jew, studied as a Jew, taught as a Jew, lived as a Jew, and died as a Jew. Jesus was never a Christian. Then I predictably hear gasps come from the youngsters who have not learned that Christianity as a religion came some years after Jesus had lived and died. They had not realized that Jesus never left Judaism. He was a teacher of the tradition which he himself is quoted in the New Testament as upholding: "I came not to destroy the law, but to fulfill it" (Matthew 5:17).

Jesus as Christ

We Jews do have some problems understanding Jesus as the Christ. The idea of a Christ is not foreign to Judaism. Christ is the Greek word for the Hebrew "mashiach," which translates into English as Messiah. Now the Hebrew word "mashiach" does not literally mean messiah. The Hebrew word means "the anointed one," and the tradition of an anointed one in Judaism goes back hundreds of years before Jesus lived to the prophet Samuel.

Samuel was called upon by the twelve tribes of Israel to appoint a man to be their king, after they had entered the promised land and settled in the areas assigned to them. The tribes needed a king because they required unity in order to occupy and defend the Fertile Crescent, the territory that they had successfully invaded. They thought of it as the promised land, promised by God to the Hebrew tribes if they fulfilled their obligations in the covenant relationship. Many nations had preceded them there, nations that were uprooted from the territory when stronger adversaries fought their way into this oasis in a vast desert. Some of these nations were prepared to fight their way back. The Hebrew tribes discovered quickly that unless they united in defending this territory, they would soon lose it. So they asked Samuel, a prophet who was recognized and respected, to appoint a king for them. Samuel opposed the idea of kingship. He feared that a king would be seen as a divine being and would replace God in their loyalties. He recognized, however, the practical reasons necessitating a king. Reluctantly, Samuel agreed to ask God to designate the man who would become the king over these tribes. Samuel prayed and found a response to that prayer in God's designation of Saul to become the first king of a united Hebrew kingdom. Samuel assembled the leaders of each of the tribes, and in their presence he anointed Saul. He placed pure oil on the head of Saul in token of God's having designated him to be king over all twelve tribes.

Samuel repeated this procedure after Saul vacated the throne. David was designated the second king by God, and anointed by the prophet. And the same thing happened with Solomon through the intercession of Zadok the priest. After that there were no more anointed kings designated by God. Following Solomon's death, the land was divided into the northern kingdom of Israel and the southern kingdom of Judea. The kings, starting with Jeroboam and Rehoboam, occupied their thrones through their military prowess. Only the three anointed kings of the united kingdom enabled the people to live in freedom in the territory that God promised to them in God's covenant with Abraham, Jacob, and Moses.

Thus it was, throughout Jewish history, whenever their freedom was threatened, whenever mighty empires overran Palestine, the Jews prayed for the coming of another anointed one, another "Mashiach," who would enable them again to live in freedom in this promised land. When Jesus lived in Judea, the Romans occupied that tiny land. It was a very cruel occupation. The soldiers were billeted in the country and were not considerate in their treatment of the natives. The taxes exacted by the Romans were a heavy burden, and the people lived in poverty and in fear. So again, in the first century of the common era, Judeans prayed for a Messiah. This was what many Jews were looking for when Jesus appeared on the scene. It seems that Jesus probably was a charismatic leader of the people, one who was respected as a rabbi, a teacher. Jesus probably attracted a following who hoped that he was the promised Messiah. But Jesus lived and died without enabling the people to overthrow the Roman rule and live in freedom. Many of his Jewish disciples no longer felt that he was the Messiah, the anointed one who would free the country. There were others of Jesus' followers who predicted his imminent return for the fulfillment of the messianic hope.

It is important to recognize that the disagreement about Jesus as Christ is not over what Jesus taught or did, but rather about what did not occur during his lifetime. Jews accept Jesus as teacher and as prophet, not as Christ or Messiah. Orthodox Jews still look forward to the coming of the "Mashiach" who will bring God's kingdom on earth with the establishment of a free Jewish nation in Palestine. The orthodox believe that will come about through a Messiah, not through political or military action. Liberal Jews interpret the prophecy still differently and look forward no longer to the coming of an individual Messiah, but rather to a messianic age, a time when all the children of God, living by God's moral law, will together establish God's kingdom on earth.

Another aspect of the Christian understanding of Jesus is also difficult for Jews. Jews do not accept Jesus as *the* son of God, but rather as *a* son of God, because Jews believe that all human beings are children of the one God. The complexities of defining Jesus as *the* son of God, and as a member of the Trinity, I shall leave to

105

Dr. Harrelson. First, though, let us consider other aspects of Jesus' relationship to Jews and Judaism in his life and in his death.

The Sadducees and the Pharisees

What was Jesus' relationship to the major political-religious groups: the Sadducees and the Pharisees? Jesus probably had very little in common with the Sadducees. They were primarily a sect whose emphasis was on Temple rituals and on the sacrificial obligations required by the priesthood. For the Sadducees, the authoritative Scriptures consisted only of the first five books of the Bible: Genesis, Exodus, Leviticus, Numbers, and Deuteronomy. The other writings were of course valuable and important, but Jews were obligated to live by the Torah, with a literal interpretation of those first five biblical books. Sadducees did not believe in the resurrection of the dead, because, they said, it was not taught in the Torah. They also were able to soften the critical words of the prophets, because the prophets did not have equal authority with the Torah, belonging as they did to later tradition.

Now, we know that sometimes the most conservative religious leaders are those who seem most easily able to collaborate with their enemies! It seems to have been true of the Sadducees too. They held fast to their idea of Torah, but then recognized that some people make adjustments to accommodate the practicalities of the "real world." And so did the Sadducees in their collaboration with Roman authorities in order to retain their own religious prerogatives.

The relationship most generally misunderstood because of misinterpretations of the New Testament passages is that between Jesus and the Pharisees. The word "pharisee" has one of two meanings: some believe that it comes from a Hebrew word meaning "separatist," that is, Pharisees were those who separated themselves from the Sadducean group. Perhaps a better interpretation is that it comes from another Hebrew word, "parisee," which translated means "to sit in the seat of Moses," that is, an authoritative teacher/interpreter of Torah. This, of course, is what Jesus was, a teacher. He was an interpreter of Torah. That was the role of all Pharisaic teachers. When Jesus came into conflict with Pharisees, as we read in the Gospels, it was an intra-group debate, not an interreligious struggle. It is the pattern that we see throughout the Talmud where many Rabbis interpret Torah from either a narrow or a broad point of view. In most areas of concern, Jesus was a very liberal teacher. In terms of observance of the Sabbath, for example, Jesus allowed his followers to gather grain on the Sabbath so that the hungry might eat. To sustain life was more important than to observe rigidly the command not to work on the Sabbath. On the other hand, there are instances in which we find Jesus stricter in his interpretation of Torah than other teachers, such as in the matter of divorce. Under certain conditions, many of the Rabbis permitted divorce. Jesus, like many conservative rabbinic interpreters of Torah, was absolutely opposed to sanctioning divorce for any reason.

When we find Jesus in conflict with Pharisees, it is as a Pharisee debating with other Pharisees as to how the Law is to be interpreted. But we find that there are many things Jesus had in common with other Pharisees. For example, Jesus probably taught in synagogues, because synagogues at this time were replacing the Temple as the meeting place for Jews to study, to pray, and to enjoy fellowship. Jesus also emphasized, as did other Pharisees, the table fellowship, where each man was a priest in his own home. It was around the table that they sat to discuss Torah and to enjoy the learning that took place at the table, as well as the fellowship. Jesus was a Pharisee who put social responsibility on a par with ritual worship. He felt that it was essential that the Law be the foundation by which people lived righteously and justly with one another.

The Essenes and the Zealots

Jesus also had a relationship with the Essenes. The Essenes are known from Josephus and from other ancient sources, and they are now much better known from the Dead Sea Scrolls. This movement arose in the middle of the second century B.C.E., not long after the rise of the Pharisees. A faithful and reforming teacher, called in the Dead Sea Scrolls the "Teacher of Righteousness" or the "Right Teacher," this devout interpreter of the Torah led a group of followers out into the wilderness of Judea, northwest of the Dead Sea, where he helped them found

107

an impressive religious community, devoted to studying Torah night and day, to living a life in strict accord with the teachings of Torah, and to preparing the way for God's coming in glory at the Last Day.

It may be that for a time Jesus joined the Essene sect, an ascetic, monastic community. If, indeed, Jesus was an Essene, this explains some things in the New Testament that are difficult for us to interpret. Consider the matter of John the Baptist having baptized Jesus. There are a number of explanations of the baptism, but a very logical one could be that baptism was an initiatory rite into the Essene cult. John the Baptist, therefore, may have inducted Jesus into the Essene cult through immersion in water for purification. Identification with the Essenes would also explain why Jesus was not married, because most Jewish men married at an earlier age. Since the average life span was much shorter in those days, we would expect that by the age of thirty-two Jesus would have been married, were he not committed at some period of his life to the monasticism of the Essene community. There was also within Jesus' teaching part of the Essene tradition that forges a mystic relationship and an intimacy with God. This is compatible, too, with what we are learning from the Dead Sea Scrolls and particularly from the Qumran community, which was probably Essene in character and philosophy.

There were other religious leaders in Jesus' day, sometimes called Zealots but also known by various other names, who found it ever harder to endure the subjugation of Israel to hated foreign overlords or to corrupt Jewish leadership. The Maccabees had provided a marvelous example of what could be done by a small but dedicated military force, with God's help. So there were "messianic" movements that arose from time to time in these years (see Acts 5:36-37), usually to be crushed rather quickly by the occupying powers or by the Jewish authorities themselves. The term "messianic" best fit these revolutionary leaders, and also those who led in the revolt against Rome in 66–70 c.e., and Simeon ben Kozibah, called by the Aramaic name Bar Kokhba ("Son of the Star"), in 132–135 c.e. It is doubtful that Jesus developed an ongoing association with the Zealots.

Jesus' Trial and Crucifixion

Our next and more difficult task is to confront the various interpretations of Jesus' trial and crucifixion. This has been one of the most controversial aspects of Jewish-Christian relationships. From a Jewish perspective, Jesus could not have been tried by the Sanhedrin or by any Jewish court for a number of reasons. There was no Jewish law that Jesus was accused of violating. Moreover, under Roman rule in Judea, the Sanhedrin had no authority to conduct civil or criminal trials. The only authority that the Sanhedrin retained was over matters pertaining to religious observance or violations thereof. Had the Sanhedrin retained the authority to hear criminal cases, it would have been governed by rabbinic law, and such a trial could never have taken place during the Festival of Passover with such dispatch. If the Sanhedrin had been empowered to try Jesus on any charge, and if a sentence of capital punishment were to have been invoked, this would have had to be publicized throughout the land, and a waiting period would have been required for any additional evidence to be heard that might exonerate the defendant. Then a second trial would have had to be held so that there would be no doubt that all evidence had been considered. Furthermore, crucifixion was the cruelest of all ways in which a verdict for capital punishment was carried out. It was a Roman method of execution, never invoked by Jewish courts.

From a Jewish point of view, only the Roman governing authority had a reason to want Jesus executed and the power to do so. Some Romans believed that Jesus threatened their control of Judea by challenging Roman patterns of governing and oppressing people. It was also a Roman custom that whenever the Jews gathered in Jerusalem for observance of the three major festivals, Rome demonstrated its authority by crucifying three prisoners. Jesus was one of those chosen for the crucifixion, perhaps since he was reported to have a large following that listened to his teachings. It may have been that some Sadducees were involved in bringing Jesus to Pilate and in urging him to pronounce the death sentence. In order to maintain their own status of priestly authority, some priests might have reported to

Pilate or to his representatives that Jesus was indeed a dangerous revolutionary, a zealot, and therefore it would be best to have him out of the way.

Paul van Buren, in his *Christian Theology of the People Israel,* summarizes this point of view so well in just two paragraphs:

> We are on more solid ground when we come to the death of Jesus. Crucifixion was the Roman form of execution especially appropriate for political crimes. If the story of the title affixed on the cross is based on fact, that is that the Romans placed over Jesus' head the words "Jesus King of the Jews," then the charge against Jesus was in fact that of treason, leading a rebellious movement intent upon replacing Roman authority with the Jewish king over Judea. Although the charge seems wide of the presumed intentions of Jesus, it would make sense in the context of much Jewish messianic hope at the time. If Jesus was in fact arrested by night and crucified the next day, his trial or hearing could not have been thorough. Pilate did not have a reputation for scrupulous attention to justice. It would have been enough for him that this unlettered Galilean was the center of a movement with messianic overtones; it would have been characteristic of what we know of Pilate to act quickly and brutally before this new movement got out of hand.
>
> The story of Jesus' arrest and of his trial before Pilate, as we have them in the Gospels, however, go out of their way to show that Jews were more responsible for the course of events than Pilate. Having been written more than 40 to 60 years after the event, their authors may have been reading back into Jesus' time the conflict which they were having with the Jewish authorities of their own day. They may also have wished to play down the role of the Roman procurator in the death of Jesus. For whatever motives, they have left the church with a story according to which Jesus went to his death because of the cries of a crowd (Mark), even of "the whole people" (Matthew), shouting, "Crucify him!" That Pilate would have bothered to consult such a crowd, much less allow the release of a murderer and rebel, Barabbas, seems utterly improbable.

The Resurrection

A more significant and a more positive link between Judaism and Christianity focuses on the climactic Christian experience: the resurrection of Jesus. Though not found in the Torah, Jewish teaching of the doctrine of resurrection goes back to the prophet Ezekiel, who wrote:

And He said to me, "Prophesy over these bones and say to them: O dry bones, hear the word of the LORD! Thus said the Lord GOD to these bones: I will cause breath to enter you and you shall live again. I will lay sinews upon you, and cover you with flesh, and form skin over you. And I will put breath into you, and you shall live again. And you shall know that I am the LORD!" (Ezekiel 37:4-6 JPS)

Scholars differ as to whether Ezekiel was describing a vision of individual resurrection or a vision of resurrection of the Temple and/or the people Israel. There is general agreement, however, that this passage definitely proclaims a belief in a tangible physical and spiritual resurrection at some future time.

This doctrine of resurrection found its way into Hellenistic teaching too. In the fourth book of Maccabees we find that Hellenistic Jewry was encouraged to remain loyal to their form of Judaism, even in the face of persecution and death. As a reward for their steadfastness, they could be assured of resurrection. It was the Pharisees, though, who made resurrection a core teaching of the Mishnah. Ellis Rivkin, in his *A Hidden Revolution,* states: "Indeed, this belief [in resurrection] is the cornerstone of the entire *halakhah* [legal] system. It was only because the true believer and true devotee of the twofold Law could hope for the immortality of his soul and the resurrection of his body that he was ready, willing, and able to yoke himself to the twofold Law and abide by its discipline" (p. 230). In several of the tractates of the Mishnah (notably tractates Peah, Sanhedrin, and Berakoth) there is ample evidence of the importance of resurrection in Pharisaic teaching. Josephus, who followed many of the doctrines of the Pharisees, also included a belief in resurrection in his *Against Apion II.* Here he asks the question as to how we can explain the loyalty of Jews to their faith even to death. Josephus finds his answer in this belief in eternal life for each individual who remained steadfast to the God-given commandments in both the written and the oral law. This faith in resurrection stripped death of its frightening power.

The belief in the resurrection of the dead became so central in

111

Jewish life that it was incorporated into the most important prayers in the Jewish liturgy, the "Shemoneh Esreh," the eighteen benedictions. The orthodox prayerbook also includes the Thirteen Principles of Faith by the twelfth-century philosopher Moses Maimonides. The last of these Principles is: "I believe with perfect faith that there will be a resurrection of the dead at the time when it shall please the Creator, blessed be His Name."

Clearly, the Christian faith in Jesus' resurrection is based on the Jewish doctrine of resurrection. For both Judaism and Christianity, belief in bodily resurrection has been a primary hope and expectation, which continues for orthodox Jews and for many Christian denominations to the present time.

UNDERSTANDING OUR RELATIONSHIP TO JESUS

A Christian Outlook

R abbi Falk has presented a Jewish way of seeing Jesus. It is my task to present a Christian perspective. While I shall attempt to present a view that is common to many Christian communities and individuals, it is inevitable that the picture of Jesus here presented will be a personal one. When one describes one's religious center of meaning, it is to be expected that the description will fail to do justice to the depths of meaning that this central reality bears. This is the case because one is straining language and imagery beyond what they can fully convey. The central Mystery of one's life remains mystery, after all the efforts to account for its essential character have been exhausted.

Religious Pluralism at the Time of Jesus

The Priestly Establishment and the Sadducees

The Jewish and Hellenistic/Roman worlds into which Jesus was born were very pluralistic indeed. In the Jewish world of Palestine there was the priestly establishment, which had exercised considerable control over the religious life of the people since the return from Babylonian exile. On some occasions, this establishment had been marked by deep commitment to the prophetic spirit and to the chief ideals of Jewish religious life (for example, in the time of the prophet Zechariah). On other occasions, as is well known from Josephus and from the books of the Maccabees, the priesthood was corrupt and was dominated by collaborators with the Persian, Hellenistic, or Roman authorities who, in exchange for personal privileges and favors, made the religious establishment an instrument of foreign control and profit.

The Sadducees

The term *Sadducees* appears in Josephus and in the New Testament as a designation for those who constitute the priestly establishment. The Sadducees were the religious conservatives of their day who, to make religion relevant to contemporary life, just separated religion and daily life! In their religious understandings and practices they were ultra orthodox. But in their actual position as leaders of the Jerusalem priesthood and of much of the political life within Israel, they could collaborate with the Persians, the Ptolemies, the Syrians, the Hasmoneans, and the Romans in turn. They took that familiar path: Let's be religious, but let's not be foolishly religious. People have after all to live in this world!

The Pharisees

Long before Jesus' time, the priestly establishment had been challenged by the Pharisees, who had with great success gained influence over the lives of the people. They had been able to break the monopoly held by the Jerusalem priesthood as interpreters of God's Torah. Arising soon after the Maccabean movement had established itself in the second century B.C.E., the Pharisees had become a very important religious and political body within the Jewish community. Their religious leaders are the ones best remembered in the Mishnah. While they are castigated in some New Testament texts for their strictness in the enforcing of the Torah, they are also clearly recognized in other New Testament texts as faithful and devout leaders of the people, persons whose entire lives are committed to making God's Torah relevant to the needs and demands of the times. Above all things, the Pharisees wanted the Torah to be Israel's guide for all aspects of daily life, a guide that all could follow, if they were ready to commit themselves unreservedly to God's cause and God's way.

The Essenes

There are remarkable similarities between the Essene community and the New Testament community. For one thing, the

Essenes believed with great confidence that the Last Days were fast approaching, when God would bring fulfillment and consummation to Israel's hopes and longings. The reason for withdrawal into the wilderness was to "prepare the way of the Lord" (Isaiah 40:3), so that God would find a faithful community living fully in accordance with the divine demands. Since life within the world of ordinary Jewish existence could not measure up, these Essenes, followers of the "Right Teacher," moved into an area in which it would be possible to live faithful lives until the time of the Consummation.

The Essenes believed in the coming of a Messiah from the line of the priests (from Aaron) and a Messiah from the non-priestly line as well. But the matters of central importance for them were faithful study of Torah, an exemplary life in communion with their Israelite colleagues, kept pure by strict discipline, and a life lived in anticipation of the Day of Consummation. In their prayers and worship they sought to anticipate the day through the sacred meals they observed regularly, through their ritual washings, and through the creation of new prayers, liturgical texts, and mystical writings expressive of their deep devotion to God, to their religious teacher, and to one another.

At the same time, the Essenes were very unlike the early Christians in some regards. John the Baptist, who seems most likely among the New Testament personalities to have spent time with these Essenes, called all Israel, and all peoples generally, to be baptized, amend their ways, and live on in their chosen professions until the Day of Consummation (close at hand) dawned. And Jesus had entirely different teaching from that of the Essenes. Those initiated into the Dead Sea Scrolls community, which was almost certainly an Essene community, were called upon to "love those whom God has elected and hate those whom God has rejected" (Manual of Discipline). Jesus may have been referring to such teaching when he said, "You have heard that it was said, 'You shall love your neighbor and hate your enemy.' But I say to you, Love your enemies and pray for those who persecute you" (Matthew 5:43-44 RSV).

It is important to recognize that many Jews in Jesus' day were not a part of any one of these three groups. They did not belong to the priestly establishment, though of course they may well have had dealings with them. They were not Pharisees, intent on the study of the Torah and the application of its provisions to daily life, though they may well have benefited from the teaching of the Pharisees. They did not withdraw from ordinary life and join the Essenes, though again, they may have admired their religious devotion or even have visited them in the wilderness from time to time.

Jesus' Relation to These Various Groups

How was Jesus related to these various groups? While it is not possible to speak with certainty, it is clear that Jesus was probably *least* closely related to the Sadducees. Jesus had little to do positively with the priestly establishment in Jerusalem, although the Gospels do show that he was not opposed to the Temple as such, nor was he indifferent to the religious festivals that had their center at the Temple in Jerusalem. The Gospel of John is organized around Jesus' visits to Jerusalem to celebrate the festivals. Jesus' theological commitments, insofar as they can be known, differed sharply from those of the Sadducees (he affirmed the resurrection, for example, and he used the prophetic texts as authoritative teaching) and of the Zealots, whom Rabbi Falk described above (Jesus strongly speaks against acts of violence even against Israel's enemies and indeed against anyone, according to much of the Gospel record).

Two main groups are left: the Pharisees and the Essenes. We have already called attention to features of Jesus' life and thought that distinguish him from the Essenes. It would appear, then, that Jesus was closest to the very group that the New Testament writings have him confronting and challenging—the Pharisees!

It is important, however, to recall that not all Jews were members of one or another of these groups. And the Zealots were not a religious party in the same way that the other three groups were. Zealots could arise from any of the three groups, or from none of them. They were persons who came to prominence out of their fierce loyalty to Israel and their conviction that the time had come to join with God's forces in ousting the hated enemy from the land. Jesus too could have been a leader of those who associated with him without thereby being identified with any of the religious or political groups. Thus, we must not place Jesus with the Pharisees simply because he is closer in thought and outlook to the Pharisees than to any one of the other groupings. Jesus could have been a popular leader with no connection with Jewish political and religious leadership at all.

One thing is clear, however. Jesus is steeped in Jewish tradition, he is a student of Torah, he knows the ways of interpretation familiar to the rabbis, and he is a master teacher and polemicist. It would be surprising indeed, therefore, if he were not associated with the Pharisaic movement in some way or other. It thus seems highly probable that, as Rabbi Falk has maintained, Jesus was a part of the liberal or left wing of the Pharisaic movement, closer to the thought and outlook of Hillel than that of Shammai (both first-century B.C.E./C.E. rabbis, Hillel being considerably more liberal in outlook than Shammai).

But Jesus seems certainly to have shared the outlook of the Essenes in one respect. He believed that the time in which he lived was close to a great Day of Consummation of God's work on earth, centered in the life of the Jewish people, centered also in Jerusalem. Over and again in the Gospels the message of Jesus unmistakably bears the mark of this exciting reality: God's rule on earth is near at hand, for God is doing decisive things to establish that rule before the eyes of the nations. Jesus' earliest message seems to have been identical with that of John the Baptist: God's rule is at hand; repent, therefore, and accept as true this Good News of God's consummation of the divine work on earth.

This message is presented not as thunderous judgment against sinners but as joy and delight that the times of suffering and deprivation and humiliation for God's people are about over. Israel is entering into an age of blessedness and peace and joy in God; it remains for Israel to prepare for this time of blessedness by its acts of repentance, its openhearted acceptance of God's coming, and its joyous waiting to see the new realities brought by God as these realities unfold. In addition, Israel is to do just what the prophets urged upon Israel in times past: begin *now* to practice righteousness; begin *now* to share life and goods with others, to extend compassion and care to all in need. The way to greet the coming of God at the Day of Consummation is *not* to withdraw from a sinful world in order to be an example to the world. Rather, one greets the coming of God by living *in the midst* of the corrupt world a life characteristic of life in the age of Consummation.

In short, Jesus agrees with the Essenes that the Consummation is near at hand. He agrees with them that radical steps are to be taken because this is so. But he differs with them as to what these radical steps are. The Essenes seek to set up an ideal community on the fringes of society, while Jesus walks among the poor and the oppressed and the struggling of his day, identifying followers from their ranks, largely, and with them looking for the Day of Consummation.

Jesus as Prophet

One of the earliest titles attributed to Jesus was that of prophet. The disciples of John the Baptist inquired whether Jesus was to be identified as Jeremiah or one of the prophets, and Jesus' own disciples grant that some say that Jesus is Elijah or one of the other prophets (Mark 8:27-30 and parallels). Jesus is presented in the Gospel of Luke (4:16-19) as having launched his ministry in Nazareth with a quotation from Isaiah 61, which was followed by Jesus' declaration that the promised day of the Spirit had now dawned. Clearly, Jesus did come to his people with the same message that Israel's prophets had brought: God demands a kind and quality of righteousness that will place Israel as a light before the nations, displaying the kind of life God desires from all peoples. But the disciples and the later Christian community found in Jesus more than a prophet.

Jesus as Teacher and Wonderworker

Jesus is a master teacher, gifted in the use of parable and simile and metaphor, steeped in the Wisdom tradition, bold in the drawing of analogies, and able to hold his own in discussions with the most learned of his opponents. Although there are parallels to most of Jesus' teaching that can be found in the rabbinical writings, it is still the case that the Gospels offer stunning

118

testimony to Jesus' gifts and powers as a teacher and an observer of daily life.

Even more impressive to the people at large is his gift of healing and his power to put to flight the demonic powers that people of his day found all around them and frequently within them. There were wonderworking rabbis in Palestine in Jesus' day, persons who had the gift of healing and who could put the demons to flight. There were also great and learned rabbis who had quite a following at the time Jesus was gathering and teaching his disciples.

It is clear, therefore, that as a teacher and wonderworker, an interpreter of Torah and a skillful and subtle applier of Torah to the situations and complexities of daily life, Jesus was close to the Pharisaic tradition, which was preserved and elaborated in the Mishnah. It is equally clear that, as one who believed in the nearness of the Day of Consummation and that radical steps were demanded by all as they confronted that day, Jesus was close to the Essenes and others (including some Pharisees) who too expected the Consummation in the near future.

But Jesus' distinctiveness did not lie in his gifts as a teacher or as a worker of miracles.

Jesus' Special Relation to God

The early Christians found in Jesus more than a teacher, more than a prophet, more than a wonderworker, more than an announcer of the Day of Consummation. Christian interpreters have often said that Jesus was a prophet, but more than a prophet; a teacher and wonderworker, but more than a teacher and wonderworker; an announcer of the Day of Consummation (the kingdom of God) and also the *bringer* of that which he announced, that is, God's very presence in ushering in the Consummation. It is in these claims of "more" that Jewish/Christian relations have often found one of their touchiest areas of difficulty.

Little is likely to be gained by the flat assertion of the divinity of Jesus by Christians, but little is to be gained by the denial of Jesus' divinity. In our discussion of the Trinity above (chapter 4) we pointed out that the Christian community comes to speak of Jesus in the language that is used of God. It was led to do so by its actual experience of the Jesus whom God (as they affirmed) had raised from death. In the earliest Christian community following Jesus' death, it was this meeting of the Jesus whom God had raised from death that led them to speak of Jesus as Messiah, as Son of God and as Son of man, as the Suffering Servant whom God had exalted.

The early Christian community combed the Hebrew Bible to find testimonies to this One whom God had raised from death to life and had exalted as Lord. Using many of the traditional passages that expressed Israel's hope in God's coming fulfillment of the divine purpose for Israel and the world, these early Christians (following a practice known in the Dead Sea Scrolls community as well) claimed for Jesus a standing with God like that given in Israel to a special creation of God called Wisdom (Hebrew *hokmâ*; see Proverbs 8, Sirach 24, and Wisdom of Solomon 7–9). This divine creation is called in Proverbs 8 the first of God's creations. She was present with God when all other created things were called into being, taking part (in some way not clearly specified) in God's creative acts. In Sirach 24 and Wisdom of Solomon 7–9, Wisdom comes forth from God like a mist or a vapor, permeating and finding a place in the totality of God's creation, so that nothing created is entirely devoid of the divine presence and character. But for Sirach and the apocryphal Letter of Baruch, Wisdom's special locale is God's Torah. In the Torah may be found the fullness of divine Wisdom.

These texts dealing with Wisdom help us understand some of the terms used for Jesus in the New Testament. In the Prologue to the Gospel of John, the divine Word is portrayed much as Wisdom was in the texts mentioned above, but the John text goes further to claim that this Word was not only present with God but was the creative agent through whom all things were made, and indeed so partook of the divine nature that the Word could also be called God. And the climax of the claim made in John 1 is that "the Word became flesh and dwelt among us" (John 1:14 RSV).

The other titles assigned to Jesus in the New Testament all, in different ways, affirm this special relationship between Jesus and God. Jesus is called Son of God, Servant of God, Messiah, and Son of man. Other titles appear as well. All of these are attempting to affirm two things at once: Jesus is a Jew, born to a Jewish mother, sharing human life fully, fully identified with humankind and with his people Israel. Jesus is also a representative of God, the One through whom God is bringing the New Age. Jesus the *announcer* of the New Age is also recognized by the early Christians to be the *bringer* of what he announced. As we noted in the chapter on God, these Christians found it necessary, from their own experience of the risen Christ, to say about Jesus, God's representative, what they said about God.

Jesus' Death and Its Christian Meaning

We noted in chapter 3 that the New Testament was produced by Christians who were experiencing the conflict between the new Christian movement and the Jewish community that had not joined that movement. The Gospels were produced in an atmosphere of frequent hostility between Christians and Jews, and they reveal the mark of that hostility especially in the stories of Jesus' betrayal, trial, suffering, and death on the cross. Rabbi Falk has noted that some Jewish authorities no doubt were involved in handing Jesus over to the Romans, but that Jesus' crucifixion must clearly be attributed to the Roman authorities, who were convinced that Jesus was involved in sedition against Rome. This conclusion seems to be the most reasonable one. The Gospel writers sharpen the conflict between Jesus and the Jewish authorities and include statements that lay responsibility on the entire Jewish people (Matthew 27:25 in particular).

But the Gospels make another very important point. *None* of those people associated with Jesus stands with him in his time of trial and persecution and death—none except the women, who seem never to have deserted him. It is not only the Jewish leaders who turn Jesus over to the Romans. Even the closest of the disciples—for example, Peter—deny that they have had any part in this movement led by Jesus. They abandon him to his death.

The Gospel writers are affirming something of immense theological importance. Jesus comes as God's very presence into the midst of a sinful world. He comes on behalf of sinful humankind and enters so deeply into the world of sin and death that sin is confronted by this very presence of God, is challenged and dethroned by One who gives his very life for the lives of those trapped by sin and marked for death. It is not that a wrathful God must be appeased because of human sin. It is that sin so claims God's good world and all its peoples and institutions and individuals that God must intervene drastically, taking the side of those trapped in sin, "becoming sin" (as Paul puts it in II Corinthians 5:21), so that thereafter this hold of sin and death on God's world is broken.

That is what Jesus' death is understood to have meant for the world. Jesus was never more triumphant, and God was never more gracious, than in the coming of this Presence of God into the world, in human form, as Jesus of Nazareth, suffering in the world on behalf of suffering humankind and dying a death that challenged the forces of darkness and death. God—so the Christians of New Testament times affirmed—took the side of humankind and brought new life out of death. The New Age is not only a time when the structures of creation are reshaped to bring peace and justice and blessing. The New Age is the age in which sin and death have been brought down, humbled and defeated, and new life bursts in upon the world as God's supreme gift to the world. Just as all, theologically viewed, participated in his dying, so all partake of God's gift of new life (II Corinthians 5:14-21).

Jesus' Resurrection

The resurrection of Jesus, experienced by small groups of Jesus' followers who had remained in Jerusalem and then by others in other locations, gives assurance to these followers of Jesus that God's message of forgiveness and new life was true. The resurrection confirmed—for them and then for the Christian community thereafter—that Jesus' life, teaching, healings, suffering, and death were what God desired of Jesus and of Jesus' followers. Christians were to live as Jesus lived, to teach and heal as he taught and healed, to face hostility and trials as he faced them, and, when necessary, to die as he died. Through the resurrection, God was affirming all that made Jesus who he was.

Viewed in this light, the resurrection is by no means a sign of

God's saving Jesus from a sinful world and removing him from all danger. And Christian salvation, therefore, is not saving individuals from sin and death and fitting them for a life with God in heaven—and nothing more. Salvation is deliverance from the hold of sin and death in order that life in this world may be what God intended that it be from the start.

Put in other terms, Jesus' resurrection is a sign that the New Age, the rule of God on earth, has come in power, but in advance of its full and public display as portrayed by Israel's prophets. The Last Day breaks in as consummation of God's purposes for all humankind, but as consummation that still awaits its final, full, and public display. Jews who accepted Jesus were able to testify to the reality of this fulfillment, this consummation, that was already present before the final public demonstration of the rule of God over the entire cosmos. Jews who did not accept Jesus pointed out that Christians were claiming too much for God's work in Jesus. Until that public display of God's consummating work on earth, one could not rightly speak of God's having fulfilled the promises made through the prophets and other leaders of Israel.

Jesus Among Jews and Christians Today

Many Christians find it quite unsatisfactory to speak of Jesus as the *only* way to life, fullness of life, with God. Exclusive claims in the name of one's own religion are hard to make and support in our religiously pluralistic world. While we need to insist that there is *one* God, we do not need to insist that *our* way to God is the only permissible way.

But the figure of Jesus claims attention throughout the world, among Muslims, Buddhists, Hindus, Jews, and persons who are not "religious" at all. Many stress the teaching and the moral example. Others also detect in Jesus one who shared life with God to such an extent and at such depth that they see his partaking of life with God as the pattern and guide for their own religious quest. To use the mystical language of the apostle Paul in II Corinthians 5, to share life with Christ is to be a new being, a new creation. Old patterns and realities fade away, and life and the world take on newness and freshness. This kind of understanding of Jesus may have little connection with doctrines

123

about the deity of Christ or Jesus' death as sacrifice for the sins of the world.

This kind of understanding of Jesus can include the idea of Jesus as teacher and healer, or Jesus as the giver of a new covenant. But its central affirmation concerns how the human community can participate more deeply in the reality of God's presence in this world. Jesus is one through whom individuals and groups enter more deeply into the divine purposes, share life with God, and work for the spread of this life in God throughout the world. Moses, then, is no rival, but one through whom one also finds the divine life disclosed. Some such move in Christian re-affirmation of the meaning of Jesus for the world seems required and appropriate in our pluralistic age.

Suggested Readings

Barth, M. *Israel and the Church.*
Borowitz, E. *Contemporary Christologies: A Jewish Response.*
Buber, M. *Two Types of Faith.*
Falk, H. *Jesus the Pharisee.*
Horsley, R. *Jesus and the Spiral of Violence.*
Isaac, J. *Jesus and Israel.*
Keck, L. *A Future for the Historical Jesus.*
Klausner, J. *Jesus of Nazareth.*
Küng, H., and W. Kasper. *Christians and Jews.*
Lapide, P. *Israelis, Jews and Jesus.*
———. *The Resurrection of Jesus.*
Pawlikowski, J. *Christ in the Light of the Christian-Jewish Dialogue.*
Thoma, C. *A Christian Theology of Judaism.*
Van Buren, P. A Theology of the Jewish-Christian Reality: Part
    II—*A Christian Theology of the People Israel.*
Vermes, G. *Jesus and the World of Judaism.*
———. *Jesus the Jew.*
Weiss-Rosmarin, T. *Jewish Expressions on Jesus.*

CHAPTER SIX

UNDERSTANDING ANTI-SEMITISM AND THE HOLOCAUST

A Jewish Outlook

> Once there was a wicked, wicked man
> And Haman was his name, sir;
> He would have murdered all the Jews
> Though they were not to blame, sir.

This first verse of a jingle, known to most Jewish children, is sung in the celebration of the Feast of Purim. The holiday is based on the story in the book of Esther in Hebrew Scriptures. Here we learn that a cruel despot, Haman, was plotting to murder all the Jews in the land (Persia?) in order to increase his political power. Haman's scheme was thwarted by the beautiful Jewish queen Esther and her uncle Mordecai. King Ahasuerus was so moved by Esther's plea for her people's lives, when she revealed Haman's nefarious plot to him, that he ordered Haman to be hanged on the gallows he had erected for the Jews.

This is the first instance of anti-Semitism in Jewish history. Though we are not certain whether this incident actually took place or whether it is fiction, the story makes us aware that anti-Semitism was a tool of racists at least 2300 years ago. This kind of political or economic scapegoatism has been exploited by tyrants throughout the centuries. In times of political turmoil or economic crisis, the Jews, who were a readily discernible minority in many lands, were blamed for the problems that beset the nation. This was the case when the Jews were exiled from England in 1290, from France in 1394, and from Spain in 1492.

In the nineteenth and twentieth centuries this pattern continued in Russia under the czars, when entire Jewish villages were destroyed. Later, under Communist rule, hundreds of thousands of Jews were executed, placed in hard labor camps, and denied the right to emigrate from this land of oppression.

Even the Jews of the United States have experienced anti-Semitism resulting from economic dislocation or political pressures. In 1654, when the first Jews sailed from Brazil to North America to escape the long arm of the Spanish Inquisition, and arrived, twenty-seven in number, at New Amsterdam, Governor Peter Stuyvesant refused to allow them to take up residence in the colony. Only through the intervention of the sponsoring Dutch West Indies Company, some of whose directors were Jews, were these immigrants allowed to remain. Stuyvesant was determined to keep them second-class citizens, though. The Jews were required to pay a special tax to provide substitute guards for themselves since the governor forbade them to stand guard in their regular turn. This restriction on their civil rights was eventually overturned in court through the efforts of Asser Levy, one of the original Jewish settlers in this new world. In most of the colonies there were laws restricting the rights of the Jews to vote, hold office, or own land. The state of Maryland repealed the last of these discriminatory statutes in 1826.

The end of discriminatory legislation did not, however, mean the end of anti-Semitism in the United States. The Depression of the 1930s saw the re-emergence of the Ku Klux Klan with its attacks on Blacks, Catholics, and Jews. There was also the vitriolic voice of Father Coughlin attacking the Jews on his weekly broadcast from Detroit. And there was Henry Ford's *Dearborn Independent* publishing the forged "Protocols of Zion," which purported to reveal a plot by Jewish leaders to control the world. The more subtle manifestations of anti-Semitism in twentieth-century America included quotas for Jewish admissions to colleges and universities, and exclusion from most fraternities and sororities on the campuses and from the country clubs in the cities. This kind of social discrimination also resulted in Jews' being excluded from the executive suites of many businesses and industries because of their inability to make the "right contacts."

Many of these manifestations of anti-Semitism disappeared during the Second World War, when people of every race and religion joined hands in combating the common enemy, fascism. The emerging prosperity also decreased the motivation for discrimination in the job market. All minorities in America began to see renewed hope for social justice and equality of opportunity in the post-war era.

Jews, however, still had another front on which to defend themselves against bigotry and prejudice. Anti-Judaism, or religious anti-Semitism, began in the first century of the common era with the missionary rivalry between Jews and early Christians, with the refusal of most Jews to accept Jesus as the promised Messiah, and with the accusations in the Gospels that the Jews were responsible for the crucifixion of Jesus. The Gospels also pitted Jesus against the Pharisees in interpretation of Torah, and made those opposed to Jesus appear to be oppressors of the people in their rigid enforcement of "the Law" and in their rejection of Christ, whose resurrection was to prepare the way for salvation for those who believed in him. Above all, though, it was the charge of deicide that made the Jews appear to be villains, absolving the Romans of any responsibility for the death of Jesus.

We can only surmise that at the time the Gospels were written, by men who did not know Jesus and who had not been present in Jerusalem in those fateful days, it was more expedient to place responsibility for the crucifixion on the Jews than on the still powerful Roman authorities, who by now were persecuting Christians with even greater intensity than they were oppressing Jews. Though there is evidence that only some of the high priestly group collaborated with Rome in plotting to kill Jesus, and though many Christian scholars today recognize that for a number of reasons no Jewish Sanhedrin could have tried and convicted Jesus of the charges supposedly brought against him, the testimony against priests, Pharisees, and the multitude of their Jewish followers has remained through the centuries as an indictment against all Jews for those who are literal interpreters of the Gospels.

Religious anti-Semitism gained momentum with the writings of the early Church Fathers and reached a heightened level of intensity when Constantine declared Christianity to be the official religion of the Roman empire in about 330 C.E. Jews, and other religious groups too, were prohibited from publicly observing their customary rituals and holiday celebrations, and from engaging in any missionary activity. Constantine set a new pattern of collaboration between secular and religious authorities in discriminating against Jews and in limiting their religious and civil freedoms.

In the Middle Ages the Crusades were the combined efforts of monarchs and church leaders to wrest control of Palestine from the Muslims. In the pursuit of this goal, though, it was the Jews who were massacred by the thousands and whose ghettoes were plundered, with the blessing of both the military and religious leaders, as the Crusaders swept through their villages. Moreover, the church leaders, with the acquiescence of the ruling monarchs, sought to convert Jews, even at the point of the sword. As Jews who refused to convert were expelled from one nation and then another, they found temporary refuge in other countries, whose rulers bled them of their material resources and then turned them out. A most vivid example of this was the Spanish Inquisition in the fifteenth century. Ferdinand and Isabella exploited their Jewish subjects to finance Spain's wars and to bolster its deteriorating economy. At the same time they permitted Torquemada to burn alive thousands of Jews on fiery platforms when they refused to convert. It was the combined strength of the state and the church that forced many Jews to become Marranos (outwardly Christian but inwardly Jews) until these Marranos also were expelled in 1492.

The most horrendous of all crimes against the Jews, however, was perpetrated by the Nazi Party under the leadership of Adolf Hitler, and with the support of some prominent Christian theologians and clergymen in Germany in the third decade of the twentieth century. One of the major issues on which Hitler rode to power was his assertion that Jews were responsible for the economic collapse of Germany at the end of the First World War. His solution to the financial bankruptcy of Germany was to confiscate Jewish property and then to make Germany "Judenrein." The German people, with a long history of anti-Semitism, responded with great enthusiasm to Hitler's campaign against the Jews. Almost immediately, upon his ascension to power, Hitler deprived the Jews of basic civil and human rights. Jews were deprived of their means of a livelihood, educational opportunities for Jewish children were limited and finally eliminated, and even respected professionals in every field found their activities severely curtailed. These economic and political disabilities were followed by the infamous Kristallnacht, when synagogues throughout Germany were looted and destroyed. Then came the concentration camps and finally gas chambers in Germany and Poland. Six million Jews lost their lives in these bestial places of torture and mass murder. Six million other human beings—Catholics, Protestant protesters, gypsies, labor leaders, and other dissidents—also were murdered. It was only the Jews, however, who were singled out for annihilation for no other reason than that they were Jews. No age in human history has ever experienced such massive genocide.

Some German and Polish Jews did find refuge in North and South America, in Europe, Australia, and Israel, but for the greatest numbers of those who sought to escape, there was no place to go. This was another unbelievable tragedy of those terrible years. England closed the doors to Palestine at the urging of the Arabs. The United States reduced the quotas of those from European countries who were allowed to find refuge on "freedom's shores." One door after another closed in the face of helpless Jewish refugees in almost every land. There were exceptions, of course. Holland accepted Jewish refugees and protected their own Jews, too, until the Nazis conquered the country. Denmark defended and aided the escape of their Jews in heroic ways. And there were individuals in every land, and many thousands working through the Underground, at great personal risk and sacrifice, who helped Jews survive. But many more Jews went down to watery graves when unseaworthy ships like the *Struma* sank with their human cargoes aboard, because they could not dock in the Haifa harbor or in Cuba or even on the Florida coast.

How could this happen in civilized, cultured nations in the twentieth century? Many sociologists, psychologists, and historians have sought to find an answer. In the play *The Deputy*, Rolf Hochhuth's thesis is that Pope Pius XII could have thwarted Hitler's war against the Jews by exerting his influence and using his good offices on their behalf. Certainly the pope could have been a more positive force in opposing fascism. And though we shall always be grateful for the hundreds of Jews, especially children, who did survive, hidden in convents and monasteries at great risk to the host priests and nuns, historians will not let us forget that had not the official Catholic Church equivocated at crucial moments they might have saved thousands more. By the same token, Arthur Morse wrote *While Six Million Died,* in which he maintained that had President Franklin Roosevelt exercised his power on behalf of beleaguered German and Polish Jewry, hundreds of thousands of lives could have been saved.

Two other men must bear significant responsibility for enabling the Nazis viciously and unrelentingly to attack human beings whose only crime was having been born of Jewish parents or, according to Hitler's racial theory, having one Jewish grandparent. William F. Albright, a prominent archaeologist and Semitic scholar during the dark days of fascism, stated in his book *History, Archaeology and Christian Humanism* that Gerhard Kittel and Emanuel Hirsch, both highly respected Protestant theologians on the faculties of major German universities, had the distinction of making extermination of the Jews theologically respectable. Albright stated on another occasion:

> In view of the incredible viciousness of his attacks on Judaism and the Jews, which continued at least until 1943, Gerhard Kittel must bear the guilt of having contributed more, perhaps, than any other Christian theologian to the mass murder of millions of Jews by the Nazis.

Robert P. Ericksen, in his book *Theologians Under Hitler,* stated that Kittel

> resurrected Christian anti-semitism from the Middle Ages, refurbished it with a touch of contemporary racial mysticism, and raised it as a German, Christian bulwark against the Jewish menace. . . . This allowed Kittel to work for twelve years within rather than outside the Party, and this physical and spiritual cooperation, whatever the limited and qualified assumptions on which it was based, was Kittel's tragic mistake. He deserves ignominy, for his writings from 1933 to 1945 were harsh and cruel. (P. 76)

Though Emanuel Hirsch and Paul Althaus, Protestant theologians who helped undergird the philosophy of the National Socialist Party, were not as blatantly anti-Semitic as was Kittel, their support of German nationalism and all that it implied provided an aura of respectability for all aspects of the Hitler ideology, including the extermination of the Jews.

Over against such figures as Kittel, Althaus, and Hirsch, were Protestant theologians and leaders like Paul Tillich, Dietrich Bonhoeffer, and Martin Niemöller, who vehemently opposed every aspect of Nazism. With great personal sacrifice and at risk of their very lives, they spoke out courageously in defense of Jews and of Christian principles that were diametrically opposed to the ugly racism and nationalism that dominated Germany under Hitler. And we do not wish to minimize the contributions of more than seven hundred Christians of at least fourteen nationalities, including Germans and Poles, for whom trees have been planted on the "Avenue of the Righteous," the sloping path that leads to Yad Vashem, the memorial in Jerusalem to the victims of the Holocaust. Undoubtedly there were many more Christians who saved Jews and provided food and shelter at great personal risk. Unfortunately, though, most Catholic and Protestant leaders, clerical and lay, were stonily silent in the face of the atrocities that were being committed in support of German nationalism.

If blame is to be assessed for the tragedy of fascism in Germany, Poland, Italy, and Austria, it is not only the political and church leaders who must bear the responsibility for the horrors that were perpetrated by Hitler and his cohorts. It was the silent "good" people who lived in the shadow of the concentration camps and the gas chambers and pretended, perhaps even to themselves, not to know what was occurring in their cities and villages. Unfortunately, this was also true in the United States. We did not want to believe that such bestiality was rampant. By our silence and inaction, we, too, were guilty of permitting six million human beings to become the victims of the worst instance of anti-Semitism that the world has ever known.

There is little doubt that anti-Semitism still exists in almost every nation in which Jews live, including the United States. There are academicians still trying to prove that there was never a Holocaust except in the propaganda issuing from Jewish sources.

There are also Skinheads and terrorists whose harassment of minorities keeps us constantly aware of the potential danger of Nazi tactics renewed by those ready to take up where Hitler left off.

Our greatest hope for successfully combating the challenges that still confront us from the hatemongers of this generation is the fact that genuine progress in Christian-Jewish relations has been made since Vatican Council II, and because of the stands taken against anti-Semitism by most major Protestant denominations. We can never afford complacency, though, nor can we cease building bridges of understanding and mutual respect, which must be the foundation for true brotherhood and sisterhood.

UNDERSTANDING ANTI-SEMITISM AND THE HOLOCAUST

A Christian Outlook

I n discussing historical perspectives above (chapter 2) we have laid out the shabby spectacle of how the Christian community has dealt with Judaism over the centuries, beginning especially at the time in the early fourth century C.E. when Christianity became the official religion of the Roman empire under the emperor Constantine. Rabbi Falk has also traced some of the particulars of anti-Semitism and the Holocaust in the preceding pages of this chapter. I wish now to make some additional remarks about Christian anti-Semitism and about Christian involvements in and reactions to the Holocaust.

The Origins of Christian Misunderstanding of Judaism

Christian misunderstanding and misrepresentation of Judaism began as the Christian community assumed its own distinct shape in the first century C.E. This occurred quite understandably and without malice, in all probability, as Christianity, a sect within Judaism, turned more and more to the gentile world and slowly laid aside its worship at the Temple in Jerusalem and in the synagogues. The process was accelerated once the Christian community had adopted Sunday as the Christian Lord's Day, the day of Jesus' resurrection, in place of the Jewish Sabbath, Saturday. In the course of this understandable separation and distancing, there crept into Christian preaching and interpretation of the Scriptures that central feature of anti-Judaism that we have pointed out frequently above. Christians began to claim that theirs was the *true* biblical religion, the authentic culmination of the purposed work of God with Israel that began with Abraham. Christian preaching made use of the Hebrew Scriptures to this end: the promises of God made to the ancestors of the people of Israel found only partial fulfillment in biblical times, but with the coming of Jesus, God indeed ushered in that fulfillment. Christianity had succeeded Judaism, and there remained no real purpose in the world for the Jewish people to serve. There can be no doubt that the heart and center of Christian misunderstanding of Judaism lies there, and there too lies the basic origin of Christian mistreatment of Jews. Put in its worst form, the argument ran: If Jews have been abandoned by God, why should Christians, now the dominant political force in the West, not do the same? The Christian theological argument, however, fastened upon the involvement of Jews in Jesus' trial, sufferings, and death, and in particular on the text in Matthew 27:25—found only in this one Gospel—that became the chief proof-text for Christians that the curse of God lay upon the Jewish people for their part in Jesus' death.

The pervasiveness of this Christian outlook is illustrated by the fact that, until very recently, many church bodies continued to hold to this view. The Jewish people, as a people, have been charged for centuries with the responsibility for Jesus' death. Biblical and historical scholarship, however, has long concluded that it was the *Roman* authorities who executed Jesus as a prophetic troublemaker and messianic pretender. Some Jewish leaders no doubt were involved, including at least one of Jesus' own disciples, Judas. But the Gospels all make it clear that, in the last analysis, Jesus died alone, supported by none of his active followers. Christian theology has seen in Jesus' dying the most graphic instance of human sin and evil, in which humankind as a whole is involved. It is the *Christian* who, in hymn and prayer and theological affirmation, says, "I crucified him!"

Nineteenth- and Twentieth-century Developments

Anti-Semitism in its modern form is generally traced to Germany in the middle of the nineteenth century, when emancipation for the Jews was granted against the opposition of such political leaders as Wilhelm Marr. Marr's opposition to equal rights for Jews in Germany came from his conviction that the Jews would always be "a state within a state," demanding concessions and advantages for themselves and refusing assimilation into the body politic. Marr was not speaking out of Christian conviction, but his own reading of Jewish history shows the same kind of prejudice against the Jews that had become a standard part of Christian reading of the Hebrew Scriptures. He says in a letter addressed to a friend and published in a Bremen newspaper in 1862 that Judaism is by nature tribalistic, incompatible with the life of the German state. There is, he says, an instinctive popular aversion to Judaism, and the Hebrew Bible indicates why: Joseph introduced slavery to the world when he was the Pharaoh's vizier in Egypt; Mordecai arranged a mass slaughter that is still celebrated at Purim; and so on. (See Moshe Zimmermann in S. Almog, ed., *Antisemitism Through the Ages*, pp. 241-54.)

The story of the rise of anti-Semitism in western Europe and in the United States has been rehearsed by Rabbi Falk above. He also has pointed out some of the specific support rendered the Nazis by Christian scholars and ecclesiastics, while also pointing out the courageous stands taken by other Christians. It is a grim and sorry story, marked by bitter and tragic ironies. At the very time when the fight for equal rights for other minorities and for woman's suffrage was being won, Hitler's Germany was making its plans to exterminate the Jewish people *simply because they were Jews*. And the Christian community was powerless to rally a majority against such a monstrous view because it had taught for centuries that God's curse lay upon the Jews for their involvement in Jesus' death, had claimed the Jewish Scriptures as their own, and found no theological reason for the very continuation of the Jewish people after the coming of Christ. The solidarity with the Jewish people that should have been a hallmark of Christianity was not to appear until *after* the Holocaust, after the death of six million Jews in the death camps, and indeed after several decades beyond the liberation of the few survivors in the camps.

The Holocaust and Its Continuing Significance

It is remarkable to see just how deeply implanted into the consciousness of a large part of the world the Holocaust has become within the several decades since the end of the Second World War. It did not happen easily. The Nuremberg trials in the late 1940s began the process of laying out the monstrous story, in the actual words of victims, onlookers, collaborators, and oppressors, as well as in the testimony of some of the chief architects of the plan to eradicate the Jewish people from Europe. Slow, painstaking work continued to document the actual events, to collect names, to secure testimony from survivors, to track down perpetrators who had escaped. Much of the world wished to forget, to leave the affair alone, but many Jews and Christians and others recognized that with the Holocaust a turning point in human affairs had been reached. Vividly before the world was an increasingly clear and inescapable picture of the depths to which human evil could go. What were the roots of this evil? Was there any logic in it at all? Or was the whole affair the irrational outcome of a deranged mind?

Holocaust studies on university campuses, state memorial acts and structures (the most notable being Yad Vashem in Israel), collections of Holocaust art, and regular commemorations of the event have established the depth of the evil, an evil that opens up an abyss for the human spirit. Studies have also revealed a kind of dreadful logic in the events that led up to the Holocaust and in its carrying through. A sufficient number of people believed in the "rightness" of this plan to destroy the Jewish people to make the plan workable. That is an unmistakable fact that cannot be denied.

It is therefore essential that the Holocaust be remembered, not only by the Jewish people, not only by the Christian communities of the world, but by all people. Hatred has led to violence in the dealings of peoples and nations throughout human history. Occasionally there have been acts of wholesale slaughter of peoples (the Armenians in Turkey in the 1915; the Native Americans during the nineteenth century in the United States; tribal groups in many lands of Africa, Asia, and Latin America; the slaughter of whole communities by Stalin; and so on). Never, however, in the history of the world has there been an instance in which the systematic mistreatment and persecution of a people has persisted over centuries, preparing the ground for the introduction of an extermination plan that very nearly succeeded. The Holocaust had many causes, but one contributing factor is undeniable: Christian misunderstanding of Judaism and mistreatment of Jews over the centuries.

"Never Again!"

Good sometimes follows evil, though it is hardly right to say that evil ever produces good. The State of Israel would have come into existence apart from the Holocaust, in all likelihood, but a shamed world was certainly ready, after the Holocaust and the struggles of Jews from Europe to get to Israel, to support the Partition Plan that led to the establishment of the state. The very existence of the State of Israel has served to help keep alive the memory of the Holocaust. The continuing conflicts between Israel and the Arab states have been reminders of how precarious is the life of this small state, a fact that immediately calls to mind Hitler's effort to exterminate the Jews and the acquiescence and indeed collusion of many in the effort. Arabs rightly point out that it was not *they* who planned and executed the Holocaust; that atrocity was the responsibility of the "Christian" West. Even so, Arab Christians and Muslims have done their part in perpetuating the Christian and Islamic ways of reading the story of the Jews. There is blame enough to go around.

Many other valuable things have happened in response to the Holocaust. The testimony of the survivors has been collected. The sheer record of the names of the victims and the survivors, the collaborators and the resisters, the helpers and the martyrs, is being painstakingly collected and studied. Research centers exist on a number of campuses and in other localities, supported by state and private funds. Lecture series are planned by Christians and Jews working together, in some instances drawn together as never before as they address this turning point in world history.

It also seems clear that the issuance of *Nostra aetate*, the Vatican encyclical that did so much to change the relations of the Roman Catholic Church and the Jewish community, followed in

139

response to the Holocaust, as did the changed attitude that was already present at the Second Vatican Council (1962–65). The Christian community should never have had in its liturgical life maledictions against the Jews for their participation in Jesus' death—but it did. The public renunciation of that way of thinking and speaking on the part of the highest authority in the Roman Catholic Church was a step of major significance.

This step had behind it the careful and patient labors of many Christians and Jews over many years. Local, national, and international committees and groups have been meeting for decades to seek better and deeper understanding of one another. Some Jews have studied Christian history, theology and ethics, and liturgy with great care in order to be better able to engage in dialogue and confrontation of the sort that has brought about this changed outlook within the Christian community. Some Christians have also studied Jewish history and literature and religious thought, including Mishnah and Gemara and Jewish mystical texts, in order to be better informed and more discerning partners in the debate.

Anti-Semitism Has Not Disappeared

As Rabbi Falk pointed out above, anti-Semitism has not disappeared from the world. Indeed, a resurgence of prejudice against Jews has appeared in several lands during the last decade. Neo-Nazi groups are predictably committed to the spread of hatred against the Jews, and such groups are in evidence in North America and in western Europe. On college and university campuses, anti-Semitic remarks are reported, from faculty members and students; and sororities and fraternities continue to exclude Jews, even though national policy of the groups is opposed to such discrimination. Country clubs and social clubs exclude Jews throughout the United States, again without having a stated policy to that effect.

Much more serious is the way in which an underlying anti-Semitic reality may be present in criticisms of the State of Israel. Here the situation is delicate indeed. Not every critical statement against policies or practices of the State of Israel is born of anti-Semitism. Any nation state in the world certainly has matters about which it can rightly be criticized. Israel is not a perfect state, and discussions within the Israeli government and press and other media reveal the depth of disagreements that there are on policies, not least the way in which the occupied territories should be administered and the question of whether land can rightly or safely be traded for peace.

It is the level and the extent of criticism of the State of Israel that may lead one to believe that there is underlying anti-Semitism present on many occasions. If Christian prejudice against the Jewish people is still being perpetuated through the church school and the pulpit and in acts of worship, not to mention theological school curricula, then this prejudice will erupt in many different ways. And if the existence of the State of Israel is one of the best ways by which the Jewish community worldwide can say "Never again!" to the Holocaust, as I think it is, then it is not surprising if Jews are edgy about unrelenting criticism by Christians of Israeli policies and practices.

Deepening Our Understanding

The most hopeful sign on the horizon is that a very sizable number of gifted artists, novelists, poets, critics, philosophers, anthropologists, and specialists in religion and theology are at work today on how to understand and address the reality and import for human existence of the Holocaust. Already, much has been done. Richard Rubenstein, Emil Fackenheim, and Elie Wiesel come to different and penetrating conclusions as to the Holocaust's import. Many religious leaders, including rabbis, priests, and ministers, note that it is impossible any longer to speak about God's guidance of the historical process in ways that had become familiar in biblical and theological studies. Some speak of the need for anthropology to take the place of theology.

Others, however, see in the Holocaust something of the depth of abysmal Mystery, where conventional moral and theological considerations seem somehow left behind. A rethinking and a resymbolization of the very structure of our religious existence is being attempted. One cannot and dare not say that the Holocaust is "producing" valuable things. But one can say that this exposure of the depths and range of human evil *may* move the human community to more productive efforts to understand life on the planet and find more telling ways to live in light of the gains in understanding that may come.

Suggested Readings

Borowitz, E. *Contemporary Christologies: A Jewish Response.*

Bratton, F. *The Crime of Christendom.*

DeCorneille, R. *Christians and Jews—The Tragic Past and Hopeful Future.*

Eckardt, A. *Elder and Younger Brothers.*

Ericksen, R. *Theologians Under Hitler.*

Flannery, E. *The Anguish of the Jews.*

Parkes, J. *The Conflict of the Church and the Synagogue.*

Peck, A. *Jews and Christians After the Holocaust.*

Roth, C. *A History of the Marranos.*

Roth, J. K., and M. Berenbaum. *Holocaust: Religious and Philosophical Implications.*

Rousseau, R. *Christianity and Judaism: The Deepening Dialogue.*

Ruether, R. *Faith and Fratricide.*

Sandmel, S. *Anti-Semitism in the New Testament.*

Yaseen, L. *The Jesus Connection—To Triumph over Anti-Semitism.*

CHAPTER SEVEN

UNDERSTANDING THE STATE OF ISRAEL

A Jewish Outlook

One of the most sensitive areas in Jewish-Christian relationships today focuses on the ways in which we view the existence of the State of Israel and its ongoing conflicts with the surrounding Arab nations. With the exception of the evangelical Christians who see in the return of the Jews to the "Holy Land" an essential prelude to the Second Coming, most Catholics and Protestants are either ignorant of, or indifferent to, the historical, theological, and political foundations of Zionism. Moreover, they are so concerned with the plight of displaced Arabs living in abject poverty and without many basic human rights that they are blinded to the hardships and the threats to survival which Israelis also endure. The purpose of this chapter will be neither to plead the cause of Israel nor to denigrate the Arabs' claims to civil rights and decent living conditions. Rather we shall seek to place the problems of the Middle East in historical perspective and then to set forth the reasons that Christians as well as Jews have a great responsibility for securing the right of Israel to exist, and for exploring initiatives they may pursue in seeking peace between the Arab states and Israel.

Perhaps it is necessary to begin by defining some of the terms we shall be using. *Zionism* is a political movement, supported by both Jews and non-Jews, whose goal has been to establish a viable Jewish state in Palestine. Paul M. van Buren reminds us that for many Jews "messianism, and not nationalism, is the primary element in Zionism." He further defines Zionism as "a peculiarly Jewish response to the secular nationalism of the nineteenth century and the trial of Diaspora existence, but its cornerstone is the conviction that Israel has been called by God to life in the land of Israel." Van Buren sees the Jewish people's independence in their own land as "a step in the direction of the fulfillment of the promise of Israel's election." *Israel* is the State which was created by the United Nations in 1948 and was thereafter recognized by almost every nation in the free world and by some of the nations in the Communist bloc. *Palestinians* are those Arabs who fled from the newly created State of Israel in 1948 when the surrounding Arab nations invaded Israel. After the war Israel would not allow the Palestinians to return to their homes, and none of the Arab nations that forced them to leave Israel would accept these refugees within their borders. These Palestinian refugees were housed in camps created by the United Nations. They were subsequently joined in these camps by Palestinians who were exiled from Jordan, Syria, and Lebanon. Many Palestinians now live outside the U.N. camps and retain ties, through families and friends, with the Palestinian communities on the West Bank and in the Gaza Strip.

The Biblical Basis for a Promised Land

Our next task is to attempt to understand both the ancient historical background of the State of Israel and the modern historical process that preceded the establishment of the State. To do this we must begin with the first patriarch Abraham, with whom God entered into a covenant that included God giving Abraham that territory over which God had control and which is known as the "promised land." Abraham had two sons: the first, Ishmael, by Abraham's concubine Hagar; and the second, Isaac, born to Abraham's wife, Sarah. Sarah was insistent that her son was the rightful heir to the birthright, which included control of that land given to this family/tribe by God. Sarah also demanded that Abraham send Hagar and Ishmael away, so that there would be no question as to the right of succession. The Bible tells us that God also provided land and protection for Ishmael, but Isaac became the son who received the patriarch's blessing and the right of succession. To this day Muslims maintain that Ishmael, whom they claim as the son through whom they are also descendants of Abraham, is the rightful heir of the patriarch and that, therefore, the promised land belongs to Ishmael's descendants (the Muslims), not to Isaac's descendants (the Jews). It is on this issue that the Muslim priests rouse their followers to take up arms to claim the land that should be their inheritance. This is a controversy that can never be settled: whether the son of the concubine or the son of the wife is the rightful claimant to his father's estate.

More important from a Jewish perspective, however, is recognition that possession of the land brings with it the responsibility to live by the commandments which are integral to the covenant between God and Israel. This is delineated so well in the eighth chapter of Deuteronomy, where we read:

> You shall faithfully observe all the Instruction that I enjoin upon you today, that you may thrive and increase and be able to occupy the land which the Lord promised on oath to your fathers. . . . Take care lest you forget the Lord your God and fail to keep His commandments, His rules, and His laws, which I enjoin upon you today . . . and you say to yourselves, "My own power and the might of my own hand have won this wealth for me." Remember that it is the Lord your God who gives you the power to get wealth, in fulfillment of the covenant that He made on oath with your fathers, as is still the case. (Deuteronomy 8:1, 11, 17-18 JPS)

Background of Modern Zionism

The fact remains that from the time of Abraham to the present day, Jews have always lived in the promised land. For only about one-third of the almost four thousand years has there been an independent Jewish state in that territory. Never, though, has there been a time when Jews did not pray for the redemption of Zion and for the opportunity to return and live at peace in this promised land.

The first major return to Palestine by Jews in modern times began in the late nineteenth century when Jews were fleeing the pogroms of czarist Russia and of equally oppressive Polish despots. This is known as the first "aliyah," the first resettlement of Jews on the land in this era.

At about the same time, a trial was taking place in France which would prove to be the impetus for calling the first Zionist congress. Captain Alfred Dreyfus was on trial before a military tribunal, accused of treasonous acts that were later proved to have been committed by one of his superior officers. The trial gained international attention, and a young Austrian Jewish reporter, Theodore Herzl, was sent by his newspaper to cover the trial. It was clear to Herzl that it was impossible for Dreyfus to get a fair trial because of the rampant anti-Semitism in the French army. Despite the efforts of outstanding Frenchmen like Emile Zola to ensure a fair trial and justice for Dreyfus, he was found guilty and sentenced to exile on Devil's Island. Herzl saw in this miscarriage of justice the continuation of anti-Semitism that would never allow Jews to live as free men and women in countries that considered them to be outsiders. Herzl, therefore, determined that the only solution to the political disabilities of the Jews was to establish in Palestine a homeland where Jews could find refuge from any country in which their liberty and their security were in jeopardy. With Herzl's call for convening the first Zionist congress in Europe, the modern political movement for the establishment of a Jewish state began.

Zionism gained momentum during the First World War when the Jewish settlers in Palestine fought on the side of the Allies, while their Arab neighbors joined forces with the Germans. In addition, toward the end of the war, an English Jewish scientist, Chaim Weizmann, developed a process for producing acetone, a solvent needed in manufacturing munitions, and gave it to the British government as a tool for speeding the end of the war. In gratitude, the British foreign secretary, Lord Balfour, asked Weizmann what he could do to honor him for this great gift. Weizmann's reply was that all he asked was that the British leaders exert their influence to hasten the establishment of a Jewish state in Palestine. Subsequently there was issued what became known as the Balfour Declaration, which stated that Great Britain viewed with favor the establishment of a Jewish state in Palestine. This was a tremendous breakthrough for the Zionists, who were also greatly encouraged when the League of Nations gave Britain the mandate to establish an independent Jewish state in Palestine. Unfortunately, the British did not fulfill that mandate. Instead, in order to gain a foothold for the empire in the Middle East, the British pitted Arabs and Jews against each other, thus making it necessary for the British to remain in control of the land. The League of Nations collapsed and with it the mandate, but when the Nazis gained control of Germany, the British were still in Palestine, cutting off Jewish immigration to Palestine at a time when thousands of lives could have been saved had that door been open for the refugees from Hitler's terror.

As a result of the tremendous contribution that the Jews of Palestine made to the Allied military campaigns, especially in North Africa in the Second World War, and because of the Holocaust in which six million Jews lost their lives in concentration camps and gas chambers, in part because there was no place to which they could escape, the question of a Jewish state in Palestine became a priority item on the agenda of the newly formed United Nations.

The Creation and Development of the State of Israel

A commission was appointed by the U.N. to explore the possible solutions to the "Jewish question" and to report to the General Assembly in San Francisco. The recommendation of the commission, to be known as the Partition Plan, was received and adopted by the U.N. in 1948. It was not a perfect solution, to be sure. It did succeed, however, in creating in Palestine an Arab state and a Jewish state, each of which already had a majority population of those who were to establish these new nations. Neither side was satisfied with the commission's recommendations. The Jews living in Palestine believed, though, that this was their best hope for finally realizing their aspirations for a state of their own. They accepted the territory assigned to them and immediately began formation of a democratic government. The five Arab states surrounding Palestine refused to accept the U.N. proposal and immediately declared war on the new State of Israel. That Israel, though greatly outnumbered and with no military supplies in any way comparable to those of the heavily armed Arabs, survived the invasion by the Arab nations, is one of the miracles of the twentieth century.

Subsequent to the 1948 war, Israel was forced to defend its borders three more times. In 1956, the Egyptians massed troops

149

on Israel's southern border and closed the Suez Canal to the ships of England, France, and Israel. In 1967 Syria, Lebanon, Jordan, and Egypt invaded Israel; miraculously Israel routed these enemies and extended its borders in just six days of fighting. Again in 1973, on Yom Kippur, the holiest day of the Jewish year, Arabs from Syria, Lebanon, Egypt, and Jordan launched a surprise attack, which Israel successfully repulsed but at a tremendous cost of lives.

The Israel-Arab Dilemma

As a result of Israel's overwhelming victory in the Six Day War, the borders of the State were enlarged by inclusion of the West Bank, the Gaza Strip, the Sinai Peninsula, and the Golan Heights. The Golan Heights remains with Israel because it was from that strategic position that Syria harassed the kibbutzim (collective settlements) that were below in the Galilee. In a dramatic breakthrough in Arab-Israeli relations at Camp David, President Jimmy Carter brought Prime Ministers Sadat of Egypt and Begin of Israel together and worked out an agreement whereby Israel would return to Egypt virtually the entire Sinai Peninsula (including potentially rich oil fields) in exchange for a promise of peace between the two nations. This meeting at Camp David was followed shortly thereafter by Sadat's visit to Jerusalem. It appeared that Arabs and Jews were finally on the road to peace. Tragically, Sadat was assassinated in Egypt not long after his visit to Israel, and though the Egyptian-Israeli border has remained quiet, little other progress has been made in normalizing relationships between the two nations.

The major unresolved problem that resulted from the Six Day War, and in part was the cause of the Yom Kippur War, is what to do with the predominantly Arab populations in the West Bank and the Gaza Strip. Even the Israelis are not in accord as to the best solution to this problem. On the one hand, the Orthodox Jews insist on keeping those two areas as part of the State of Israel, because these were the territories known as Samaria and Judea in biblical times, and therefore are integral parts of the land that God covenanted to the Hebrews. On the other hand, equally vehement Israelis recognize that to keep the West Bank and the Gaza Strip as part of Israel would mean that in a very short time the majority population in Israel would be Arab, and the cherished dream of a Jewish state would vanish. Furthermore, many Jews recognize the importance of self-government and civil rights for Arabs as well as Jews. The grave concern of Israelis is that if an independent Arab state were created on the West Bank or in the Gaza Strip, a potential enemy would be but a few miles from Jerusalem and within easy reach of the other population centers in Israel. This would give the Israelis virtually no warning time if another surprise war were to be launched by Arabs from those territories. Israel is caught on the horns of a terrible dilemma, and no one, within or outside of Israel, has been able to produce an equitable solution. Israelis and their supporters realize that time for finding answers is running out. The constant skirmishes between Palestinians and Israeli troops are both wearing and demoralizing. Even more crucial is the fact that with the Soviet Union's help Syria is gaining military strength and could soon be a formidable enemy on the northern border, at a time when Israel is being weakened by the conflict with Palestinians and by the internal conflict between Jews in the two major political parties.

The Jewish-Christian Breach

Adding to the uneasiness of the Israelis is the fact that only the United States, of all the major nations of the world, supports Israel both politically and economically. Even in the United States, though, the support of the organized Christian communities, with the exception of the evangelicals, has been either token assistance or none at all. This was especially alarming during the Six Day War in 1967. Once again, Jews were confronted with a war that threatened genocide, because the announced intention of the Arab world was to drive all Israelis into the sea. In the early days of that war, it seemed that the Arab threats would be carried out successfully. Yet, despite the importunings of American Jews and Jews throughout the world, the Christian churches and the Christian nations remained harshly silent. This re-opened a wide breach in Jewish-Christian relationships that had been carefully cemented through the years. Finally groups and individuals from both sides began discussing this issue of the role of Christians in the critical quest for survival of the Jewish state. This resulted in more Christian support for the defenders of Israel in 1973, but even then the support of organized Christian denominations was minimal.

Jews understand that part of the reluctance of Christians to come to the aid of the State of Israel has been the close ties many Christians have formed with Arabs through their foreign missions and through the American universities in Arab lands that are supported by Christian institutions. Jews also understand the justifiable concern of many Christians for the Arab refugees who languish in the U.N. camps, and who presently have no homeland of their own. It does seem strange to Jews, however, that Christian spokespersons can be so vehement in their demands that Israel assume responsibility for resettlement of the Arabs, ignoring the obligations of both Syria and Jordan to resettle the much larger numbers of Arabs who are in those same refugee camps because they were forced to leave their homes in both of those Arab nations. In Jordan, the Palestinians had been a majority population before they were forced to leave their homes there.

Jews are also bewildered by the fact that Christians have such compassion and concern for Arab refugees, and seemingly feel no responsibility for the population of Israel, virtually all of whom are also refugees. Many are the survivors of Nazi concentration camps in Germany, Poland, and France. Many more Jews in Israel today, though, are refugees who fled persecution in their native Arab and African lands to find some haven of hope in Israel. Why have Christians felt no compassion for Israel's refugees from Arab lands and from Europe's fascist nightmare? And why have American Christians been so indifferent to the tragedy of Christian Arabs who are being massacred daily by Muslim Arabs in Lebanon? Are Christians interested only in placating third world nations who insist on regarding the wealthy Arab nations as underdogs in their conflicts with Jews? Are not the Israelis the real underdogs in the Middle East? They cling desperately to a homeland not as large as the state of Vermont, supported only by the United States and Diaspora Jewry, surrounded on every other side by real and potential enemies threatening total annihilation. Is it possible that the anti-Israel stance of many Christian leaders and their followers is really anti-Semitism by another name? Jacques Maritain, the noted Catholic philosopher, answered these questions when he wrote: "To wish to reject into nothingness this return which finally was accorded to the Jewish people, and which permits it to have a shelter of its own in the world . . . is to wish that misfortune hound again this people, and that once more it be the victim of iniquitous aggression. Anti-Israelism is not better than anti-semitism" (Rousseau, *Christianity and Judaism*, p. 161).

The Relationship of American Jews to Israel

It is also possible that the Christian world has never really understood the multi-faceted relation that Diaspora Jewry, especially American Jewry, has with the State of Israel. There are some extreme orthodox Jews, for example, who do not accept the existence of a Jewish political state in Palestine, because they insist that redemption of the promised land cannot be realized until the Messiah comes. These orthodox, therefore, do not recognize the authority of the government of Israel, will not serve in the armed forces of the State, and will not even speak Hebrew, the official language of the State. At the other extreme are the Jews who, especially prior to Hitler, were anti-Zionists. They felt that the mission of the Jews would be fulfilled only as Jews remained scattered among the nations to bring God's Word to all humankind. However, the Nazi nightmare in Europe converted most non-Zionists and anti-Zionists into strong political and philanthropic supporters of Israel. They recognized that for Jews who were oppressed in the countries of their sojourn there had to be found a land ready to accept them as citizens, entitled to the same civil rights that all other free people enjoy.

The vast majority of American Jews feel that their roots in the United States are much too deep for them to wish to emigrate to Israel (that is, to make aliyah). Many American Jews are descendants of pioneers in this new world, and they have no desire to move to Israel. This is something that most Israelis do not understand and is the cause of some conflict between

American and Israeli Jews. Nevertheless, if American Jewry is to be remembered for any achievements in centuries to come, we will be remembered as the most generous community in history because of our unstinting support, even at times sacrificial support, for our fellow Jews in Israel.

Israel is important to American Jews and to world Jewry not only as a refuge but as the fountainhead of our Jewish cultural, educational, and spiritual resources. For all Jews, it is still the land of promise, the land that is a fundamental part of our covenant with God. It is the focal point of our sense of peoplehood.

When Jews proclaim *"Never again!"* we do not only mean that never again will we allow the tragedy of the Holocaust. We also mean that never again will there be a time when there are no doors open for the escape of Jews from lands of oppression. We mean never again will Jews be content without a voice in the council of nations. We mean never again will we forget our covenant with God which challenges us that "instruction shall come forth from Zion, the word of the Lord from Jerusalem" (Isaiah 2:3 JPS).

The Unfinished Tasks and the Goals of Israel Today

The goal that all Jews cherish for the State of Israel can be simply stated: a free, democratic state, living at peace with its neighbors and with all nations. There are, however, significant differences in the ways in which we believe this goal can be achieved. The central issue is how best to deal with the territory of the West Bank and the Gaza Strip and how to solve the problem of the Palestinians living in those areas. One of the major political parties in Israel, the Likud, believes that those territories are integral parts of the covenanted land from biblical times and must remain a part of the present State. They believe that the Palestinians should be given certain autonomy but not independence, because of the potential military threat of another Arab state so close to the major population areas of Israel. The other major political force in Israel, the Labor party, is much more willing to make major land concessions, as was done with Egypt at Camp David, in order to achieve peace. They recognize, however, that Israel cannot solve the problems of the Palestinians alone, but must do so in concert with neighboring Arab states, namely Jordan and Syria, and with the support of the other Arab powers in the region. Thus far, no Arab state, other than Egypt, has indicated any willingness to participate with Israel in confronting the problems and alleviating the misery of the Palestinians.

The vast majority of American Jews are deeply concerned that solutions be found now for the plight of the Palestinians. We recognize, however, that this can be done only as part of a plan that will bring peace to Israel and its surrounding Arab neighbors. We also know that Israel cannot achieve these goals alone. Israel needs both the cooperation of the so-called moderate Arab states and, even more, the understanding and support of the Christian world.

The conflict between Jews and Christians regarding the Christian world's relationship to Israel has been a source of great pain and sorrow for both Jews and Christians of good will. In the Introduction to his book *Christianity and Judaism: The Deepening Dialogue,* Richard W. Rousseau, S.J., summarized this problem best when he wrote:

> There are many Christians who seem embarrassed by Jewish claims to the land and the State of Israel. Though they fully support claims of spiritual and religious freedom and though they express horror at any active persecution of the Jews, they often seem confused when all this turns into the flesh and blood (sometimes bloody) realities of the land of Israel and its wars of self-defense. Though there are many political reasons undergirding the State of Israel, including the continued presence there of Jews from the time of the First Exile, the religious reasons are most important and Christians should be sensitive to these religious reasons.
>
> One of the purposes of Jewish-Christian dialogue, then, should be to clarify these issues concerning the State of Israel, so that, both sides being basically satisfied, the dialogue can then move on to more immediately religious and spiritual issues. (P. 23)

We join Father Rousseau in this hope that Jews and Christians can seek and together find a common ground on which to build firm support for the State of Israel, and at the same time join in the quest for securing basic human rights for the Palestinians. Only then can we feel that Jews and Christians together are contributing to freedom and enduring peace for Israelis and Arabs in the Middle East.

If this goal is to be achieved, and the State of Israel is to become a true beacon light of justice not only for Arabs and Jews but for all nations, it must begin with the recognition that Zion is more than physical space. It is, as Walter Brueggemann put it, "space in which important words have been spoken which have established identity, defined vocation, and envisioned destiny. [This] place is space in which vows have been exchanged [between God and Israel], promises have been made, and demands have been issued." Faithfulness to the vows and demands of the covenant established in this promised land is the only real hope for fulfillment of Israel's witness to the land as the land of Torah, the land in which God's moral Law is taught and in which God is worshiped through the words of our mouths and the deeds of our hands.

UNDERSTANDING THE STATE OF ISRAEL

A Christian Outlook

Land in the Hebrew Bible: An Overview

Life began for the first human pair in a garden stocked with all that human life required—the gift of a good and gracious God. And the promise of God to Abraham included a promise of land. The emphasis falls not on the land as such (Genesis 12:1-3) but on the family that God will raise up for Abraham, and upon Abraham's destiny to bring blessing to all human families. Even so, the land is clearly a part of the promise.

Soon, the land will stand out more prominently. Famine comes, in this land destined to be the scene of Abraham's blessing from God, but the trek into Egypt ends with riches and blessing, and the land recovers from famine. But again famine strikes, this time with devastating force on the entire region, including Egypt as well as Palestine. But once again, God has provided a way out: Joseph had been sold into slavery by jealous brothers, but the end result was his rise to prominence in Egypt, where he was able to spare the lives of many Egyptians when the famine struck, while also being in a position to spare the lives of Abraham's descendants and maintain the divine promise to Abraham.

But again, disaster strikes, and this time it is the act of human oppression that almost brings God's promise to nothing. God's people are cruelly enslaved and their very existence is threatened by measures designed to blot them off the face of the earth. God hears their outcry, determines to come to their aid, and raises up Moses and Aaron to lead them to freedom.

In this context, the land looms large once more. Egypt, the great empire with its Pharaoh as a divine king, is no place for freedom to flourish. It is a place where masters lord it over subjects, where the lives of most people are given over to caring for the life and comforts of the few. Israel must have its land, its equivalent of that garden first planted by God for the first human pair. The phrase is created, "a land flowing with milk and honey" (Exodus 3:8 is the first occurrence of the phrase), a clear indication of how important the land of the promise is becoming.

The land is more and more idealized, identified as the source of great fertility and rich resources of iron and copper (Deuteronomy 8:7-10), of abundant water and flowing streams. This idealization reaches its height in the prophetic and cultic texts describing Mount Zion, the height on which Jerusalem is built. Beneath the mountain lies the source of vast waters, now coming out only in small quantities through the Gihon Spring, but destined in the future to burst out and flow to east and west, sweetening the waters of the Dead Sea itself, and gushing out to empty in the Mediterranean in the west. Anglers will gather along the banks to catch fish; trees will grow up to provide fruit and shade (Ezekiel 47:1-12; Zechariah 14:8).

This idealization applies to the whole earth as well, as we can see in Psalm 104 and in other texts portraying the divine creation. The earth was provided with every good thing and every necessity for all its creatures. While Palestine is clearly the model for the portrayal of earth found in Psalm 104, the author's thought applies to the creation as a whole. God provided the mountains on which the earth is anchored, the seas that teem with life and support the ships afloat on them, the land that touches the sea but is not any longer threatened by the sea, since God has fixed its bounds permanently.

Streams flow from the mountainsides, creating rivers that pass on into the seas. Beside the streams, trees grow and spread their branches. Birds nest in the branches and sing their songs. Fields stretch out to receive the seeds that farmers plant, and earth produces abundantly for human and other creaturely need. Wild animals have their domain in the rocks and the crags where no one disturbs them; the night is the arena for the beasts of prey to roam and get their food from God's table.

This marvelous hymn in praise of the God of the natural world enables us to see how ancient Israel viewed land. It is an absolutely indispensable reality; who can possibly live without land? And it is the sheer gift of grace to *all living beings,* not to Israel alone. It is in this context that the promise of a land for Abraham and for the freed slaves from Egypt should be placed. Land is a gift of God to all; a particular land is God's special gift to the people of the covenant.

The Land as a Trust from God

In our discussion of election and covenant we will see that God's choice of Israel was understood to have arisen out of the sheer mystery of divine grace. Explicitly denied is any notion that the people of Israel *deserved* the land because of some virtue or merit that lay within them. Deuteronomy is most explicit: it was because God loved Israel and because of God's promise to Abraham, not because Israel was the greatest of peoples or the most virtuous (Deuteronomy 7:7-8). This same point applies, of course, to God's gift of the land of Canaan.

Efforts in ancient Israel to explain how the land, then occupied by others, could have been turned over by God to Israel were no more successful than contemporary efforts. Some passages claim that the Canaanites, because they worshiped idols and practiced abominable religious rites, had forfeited any right to continue to occupy the land. Throughout the centuries and up to our own day, some historians and theologians have claimed the same. It seems unlikely that such a philosophy of history can account for the rise and fall of nations. Moral decadence does, of course, frequently contribute to the fall of a culture or a civilization. But more important, usually, is the appearance of another people on the scene, eager for its chance and ready to risk all to claim a given locality for itself.

The remarkable fact about the Hebrew Bible's portrayal of God's gift of the land to Israel is its set of built-in safeguards against pride and arrogance ("my power and the might of my hand have gotten me this wealth," Deuteronomy 8:17 RSV) or against the betrayal of the divine covenant on which the gift of land depends. Over and again, the leaders and prophets of Israel called on the people to bear in mind that the land was "being given" to Israel (the Hebrew uses the participle *noten* with the meaning to grant as a trust, to give over contingently). It was *God's* land, which God was *granting in trust* to the descendants of Abraham. Israel was to practice justice in the land, display devotion to God, and show concern for the rights and needs of others. Otherwise, the land could be withdrawn, along with other divine blessings.

Israel's prophets spoke with great ominousness of the likelihood of the loss of land as a result of Israel's failings to hold fast to the covenant. And when, finally, the land of North Israel was taken away by Assyria in 722/721 and Judah fell to the Babylonians in 597 and again in 587/586, prophets and psalmists alike acknowledged that Israel had come to ruin as a result of its sin.

Christian Misreading of Israel's Sin

At just this point, however, it is important to recall how Christians have misused this judgment upon Israel that was pronounced by *Israel's own leaders and prophets and psalmists.* We Christians often have read the history of biblical Israel as a history of continuing and stubborn apostasy from God, fully justifying God's judgment upon them through the loss of the land and the other calamities that have befallen God's people through the centuries. How easy it has been for Christians to take these confessions of sin and turn them into factual statements! When that is done, the entire history of Israel is read in a way that favors the Christian community and trivializes the theological judgments of Israel's leaders and prophets. It was Israel's own leaders who insisted that God demanded faithfulness in keeping the Torah; without faithfulness, God's promises of land and people and a rich future could not be expected to stand.

The same prophets and leaders, however, also stressed that the God who demanded strict justice from Israel also understood the frailty of humankind and the disposition of individuals and communities to turn from God and from their true good. These same prophets and leaders spoke of God's extraordinary mercy toward humankind, of a love for Israel not blotted out when

Israel did not measure up to the demands of covenant. And thus, just as election and covenant were marked by God's unfailing mercy toward sinners who confessed their sins, so also God's promise of the land was a promise extended out of the merciful heart of God.

The Land: Central to God's Future Promise

It is often overlooked that the future promised to Israel and the nations is also tied to this gift of the land. One of the earliest promises, dating to the tenth century B.C.E., speaks of a ruler who will arise from the tribe of Judah (Genesis 49:8-12) and exercise authority over the surrounding peoples. His reign will be marked by prosperity and plenty, and he himself will be a sign of this age of plenty. His teeth will glisten from the abundance of milk available to be drunk, and his eyes will sparkle from the abundance of wine at hand. At the end of the words of the prophet Amos (9:13-15) is a similar portrayal of this age of plenty. A day is to come when the one who plows will overtake the one who reaps the harvest, when the one who treads out the grapes will be at work before the one who plants the seeds. One harvest will follow upon another with such rapidity that the scourge of famine will be obliterated forever.

Other prophetic pictures of the Day of Consummation are similar. They show that the deepest hope and longing of Israel's leaders was for a day when the basic necessities of life would be available to all: all would have food and drink, clothing and shelter, work and hope for the future. Sometimes the texts spoke of the end of warfare and the establishment of peace among the nations (Isaiah 2:2-4; 9:1-7; 11:1-9; Micah 4:1-4; 5:1-5a). Sometimes they portrayed worship at Jerusalem that brought all the nations to this center of the universe (Zechariah 14:16-21). Sometimes they described the creation of a community of nations with its center in Jerusalem (Zechariah 2:6-13; 9:9-12). But all of these promises that dot the pages of the prophetic texts speak of fulfillment of God's promises on a transformed earth, on the land that God has created and sustained throughout all trials, on land that usually, though not always, has as its center the land that God granted to Israel, the land called Israel or Palestine.

161

In our day we have come to see more clearly the significance of land for the life of every human being. Land is a symbol for the need to have a place to which one belongs, a place that can be called home. Today, boat people and refugees from many lands undergo extraordinary hardships in order to reach a land that can become home, when their traditional home has become intolerable for them. City life often robs some of its citizens of any place that can be called home. The term "homeless" means much more than the loss of living quarters; it means a life without roots, without direction, aimless, with even history seemingly blotted out.

In our day the tragedy of landlessness has loomed larger than ever before as the world's citizens have come to see how unequally divided are the resources of God's earth. In some lands, 10 percent of the population control and reap the fruit of 90 percent of all the land. In many lands of the west and of the Pacific Rim, a few million of the earth's population live in extraordinary comfort, if not luxury, while the hundreds of other millions struggle merely to survive, living at the very margin of sheer existence. Clearly, biblical faith intends no such unequal distribution of the earth's land and riches.

Land in New Testament Perspectives

Is land as important for the Christian community as it was and is for the Jewish community? Most Christians would probably say no. "Our commonwealth [Greek politeuma] is in heaven," the apostle Paul can claim (Philippians 3:20 RSV), and many Christians through the centuries have viewed earthly life as but a pale shadow of the life to come with God in heaven and have seemed to denigrate and play down the importance of this earth. With such a view of earthly existence, the promises of land and of earthly fulfillment—so richly in evidence in the Hebrew Bible—seem to have little place.

The Christian inheritance promised by God (Greek kleronomia) can even be contrasted with the early promise of inheritance to Israel (I Peter 1:4; Hebrews 9:15; 11:8). This understanding of God's promise of land and blessing is not, however, sharply in contrast with the view found in the Hebrew Scriptures at all. The

Christian claim, once more, has to do with how close the community of faith is to the Day of Consummation. Christians are claiming that what God promised is already near at hand, able to be claimed, and therefore seized now, in faith, before it is publicly displayed and visible to all.

There can be no doubt, then, that Christian understanding of the fulfillment of God's promises does change the attitude that Christians have toward the land of the promise, toward Jerusalem as a concrete geographical locality, toward a single plot of ground. Such promises as Ezekiel's picture of a day to come when all the tribes of Israel will occupy allotted portions of Palestine, with Jerusalem and its religious personnel occupying the central portion (Ezekiel 47–48), have always, or almost always, been secondary in Christian history.

The Land in Christian History

It is remarkable that the churches that flourished most prominently in Christian history after the first century were not in the Holy Land. Alexandria, Antioch, and Rome became churches of central importance for the Coptic, the Syrian, and the Roman churches respectively, while Jerusalem remained of great significance for the Greek world, later to be overtaken in importance first by Caesarea and then by Constantinople. Even so, the Holy Land was of very great significance for the entire Christian world, as a place to which the Christian soul was drawn as it heard the biblical lessons read, as it followed in Christian study and worship the path of its Lord to Jerusalem, and as indeed the entire sweep of Christian liturgical worship traced the path of Jesus from birth in Bethlehem, upbringing and early ministry in Galilee, teaching and healing throughout the Holy Land, and suffering, death, and resurrection in and around Jerusalem.

Christian pilgrimages began early in the history of the church; and, even prior to the stream of Christian pilgrims from the West, Greek and oriental Christians regularly made their way to the Holy Land, with literally thousands of Byzantine Christians settling in the land and building churches and communities in all possible localities. A Christian community has been in the Holy

163

Land since the beginnings of Christianity. Today, Greek Orthodox and Catholic Christians proudly affirm their identification with the earliest Jerusalem church.

In addition, many Christian religious communities have sent their representatives to the Holy Land from churches throughout the world, establishing churches and religious orders there to maintain a presence in this land of the birth of Christianity. Crusaders no doubt had mixed motives as they made their marches to the land of the Bible, some seeking adventure and plunder, some bent upon freeing the holy places from occupation by the Muslims, and some motivated largely by the drawing power of the sacred sites.

All such motivation, however, falls short of the kind of connection that Jews have felt for the Holy Land. Christianity, through its understanding of the consummation of the divine purpose that has dawned in Jesus Christ, thinks in universal terms. All places and localities are suitable places for the practice of Christian faith, though the land of the birth of Judaism and Christianity has had its strong hold upon the Christian heart. For the Jewish community, however, the land has a distinct place that Christians ought to understand very well, even if they do not entirely share that understanding.

Zionism and the State of Israel

Rabbi Falk has laid out the story clearly and well above. Let me only add a word about Christian responses to Zionism and to the State of Israel. The first point is to note that the Christian presence in the Holy Land has also been continuous since the beginnings of Christianity, just as the Jewish presence has been continuous since at least the time of Joshua (about 1200 B.C.E.). The existence of Christian communities and of Christian religious orders in the Holy Land has colored the attitudes of Christians toward Zionism and toward the establishment and later history of the State of Israel.

Many Western Christians, however, have not found themselves drawn in special ways to the indigenous or ancient Christian churches of the Holy Land. More important to them have been the Western establishments in Palestine: the Western Catholic religious orders and the Western Protestant missions and educational and archaeological institutions. Sympathy in the conflicts between Jews and Arabs has frequently been extended to the Arabs by the Western Christians, both because their establishments and institutions have been located among the Arabs, especially the Arab Christians, and because of the anti-Jewish element that has been so prominent in Christianity through the centuries, as we have seen.

The result has been that the establishment of the State of Israel has received stronger endorsement by the political voices in the West than it has by the religious voices. Only among those Christian bodies that have seen in the establishment of the State of Israel a sign of the nearness of the Second Coming of Christ has there been strong and enthusiastic endorsement of the State of Israel by Christians. Such endorsement has a certain irony about it: these Christian bodies are the ones most likely to pursue a "Christian mission to Israel," seeking to convert Jews to Christianity. And the theological anticipation held by many such groups is of a Consummation when the Jews will be converted to Christianity and Judaism will cease to exist.

Nonetheless, it is good to see that within evangelical Christianity there has been, through the decades of the existence of the State of Israel, such a solid and dependable affirmation of Israel's right to exist, and such regular political support for Israel during its struggles to defend itself against those who have repeatedly called for the state's annihilation. By contrast, non-evangelical Christianity has been much less dependable, much more ready to support the Arab cause alone.

In recent statements by Christian bodies, this lack has begun to be remedied. Very careful statements have been adopted that point to the religious significance of the land of Israel for the Jewish people and to the right of Israel to be enabled to exist in its land, with secure borders, and at peace with its neighbors. Such statements do not specify that the promise of God to Israel's ancestors entitles Israel to claim the land as its own as a political right that all nations should respect. Such a mixing of the theological/religious and political approaches to the State of Israel would be quite inappropriate and would not be welcomed by most citizens of Israel. Such statements also go on to affirm, as

165

most citizens of Israel also affirm, the rights of the Palestinians to justice in their land, to a place they can call home, and to security from mistreatment by their neighbors.

It is clear that the situation in Israel and in the occupied territories is very serious and urgent indeed. Israel has to take such actions as are necessary to secure the lives and welfare of its citizens and visitors to Israel. The Palestinians cannot much longer be denied a tolerable level of justice; they cannot forever live their lives under the domination of occupying forces, with no rights of self-determination.

It is a remarkable achievement of the State of Israel that throughout over forty years of existence, during which it has never been permitted to live at peace with its neighbors, the state has been, on the whole, a champion of public justice and of the rights of its individual citizens, while it has opened its doors to Jewish refugees from around the world. It is a remarkable achievement that Jews the world over, and non-Jews and many Western governments and foundations and enterprises as well, have contributed to the maintenance of this democratic state, where finally, after millennia during which the people of Israel have had to find citizenship in such states as would extend it, the Jewish people have a state of their own.

It is true that this achievement has been at considerable cost to Palestinians who have lost land and goods and dignity during the endless conflicts of these forty years and more. None knows this better than the citizens of Israel themselves. It is also true that injustices continue to be perpetrated on both sides. But the achievement stands: freedom of expression, struggles for justice and equity, and hopes for a resolution of the conflicts still animate this young state.

Christian approaches to the State of Israel still require continuing reflection, debate, and restatement. Some of the church bodies remain silent. The Vatican still has not recognized the State of Israel. But a fresh impetus is present and unmistakable.

Suggested Readings

Eckardt, A. R. *Elder and Younger Brothers.*
Lapide, P. *Israelis, Jews and Jesus.*
Oesterreicher, J. *Brothers in Hope,* vol. 5.
Talmage, F. E. *Disputation and Dialogue,* Parts IV and V.
Van Buren, P. A Theology of the Jewish-Christian Reality: Part II—*A Christian Theology of the People Israel.*

CHAPTER EIGHT

UNDERSTANDING ELECTION, COVENANT, AND MISSION

A Jewish Outlook

God's election of Israel is the foundation for everything that Israel has to say and for its continuing existence as his witness. Everything else in Israel's life and testimony follows from this; nothing precedes or leads up to it. Israel is the people of God or it is nothing." Thus does Paul M. van Buren summarize the vital importance of election as the foundation upon which Israel enters into covenant with God (vol. 2, pp. 116-17).

Throughout Hebrew Scriptures our prophets and sages emphasized the covenantal relationship of God and Israel. So basic was this relationship to their way of life that the covenant of God and Israel was often compared to the covenant established between man and woman in marriage. In chapter 54 of the book of Isaiah, this husband-wife covenantal relationship of God and Israel is beautifully described:

> For He who made you will espouse you—
> His name is "Lord of Hosts";
> The Holy One of Israel will redeem you,
> Who is called "God of all the Earth."
>
> The Lord has called you back
> As a wife forlorn and forsaken.
> Can one cast off the wife of his youth?
> —said your God.

> For the mountains may move
> And the hills be shaken,
> But my loyalty shall never move from you,
> Nor My covenant of friendship be shaken
> —said the LORD, who takes you back in love.
> (Isaiah 54:5-6, 10 JPS)

The first two chapters of the prophet Hosea have been interpreted by many biblical scholars as being an allegory in which God is the husband and Israel is God's faithless wife. The climax of this relationship of God and Israel comes with a delineation of the essence of this marriage covenant:

> And I will espouse you forever:
> I will espouse you with righteousness and justice,
> And with goodness and mercy,
> And I will espouse you with faithfulness;
> Then you shall be devoted to the LORD.
> (Hosea 2:21-22 JPS)

Marvin Wilson also reminds us in his book *Our Father Abraham* that "the rabbis regarded the Jewish marriage service as reflecting the main features of God's covenant with Israel at Mount Sinai. The covenant ceremony of marriage was seen as a replica or a reenactment of what happened at Sinai. It was designed to be a reminder of that basic covenant obligation which binds God to His people" (p. 203).

God's Covenant with Abraham

Having established the centrality of election and covenant in Jewish thought, we now turn to the historical development of these relationships with our patriarchs, with the promised land, with Torah at Sinai, and with the Jewish people. Our introduction to the first patriarch, Abraham, is the announcement of his election by God in chapter 12 of Genesis:

> The LORD said to Abram, "Go forth from your native land and from your father's house to the land that I will show you.

170

> I will make of you a great nation,
> And I will bless you;
> I will make your name great, . . .
> And all the families of the earth
> Shall bless themselves by you."
> (Genesis 12:1-3 JPS)

This election does not come to Abram by reason of his merit. There is nothing in the biblical story that provides any reason for Abram's having been elected by God.

Only with the Rabbis in the Midrash do we find an explanation offered for the election of Abram. In Midrash Rabba to Genesis, we are told that Abram was chosen by God because of his rejection of the idols of his father, Terach. Abram smashed the idols in his father's workshop as proof that these man-made images were weaker even than mere humans. Abram then left his father's house so that his worship of the unseen deity would not be contaminated by the idolatry of his father. This explanation does not appear in Hebrew Scripture, however; therefore we must conclude that, for the author(s) of Genesis, Abram's election was not because of his merit but by divine grace. The author(s) of Genesis also make certain that we recognize that the election was not only of Abram, but also of the generations that would follow him: "I will maintain My covenant between Me and you, and your offspring to come" (Genesis 17:7 JPS).

One more essential aspect of the election of Abram and his descendants is found in these early chapters of Genesis. The purpose of the election of Abram is not just for the sake of the people Israel, but is for the good of all humankind: "And all the families of the earth shall bless themselves by you" (Genesis 12:3b JPS). This concept of the election redounding to the benefit of all humankind is integral to the universality of the outreach of Israel's sages. The theme of the universal mission of the Jews recurs throughout Torah and the writings of the prophets. It is important, though, to see that the calling of the first Hebrew includes this challenge to fulfill Abram's relationship with God not just for his own sake, or for his descendants, but for all the children of God.

God's Election of the Jewish People

Moving on from the election of Abraham and his descendants to the broader concept of the election of the Jewish people, we find the relationship of God to this chosen people most clearly stated in the book of Exodus: "Now then, if you will obey Me faithfully and keep My covenant, you shall be My treasured possession among all the peoples. Indeed, all the earth is Mine, but you shall be to Me a kingdom of priests and a holy nation" (Exodus 19:5-6a JPS). On what basis was this Hebrew tribe chosen to be a kingdom of priests and a holy people? It is important to underscore the fact that it was not as a reward for special merit. Nor would this election raise the Hebrews higher than others in receiving God's favor or compassion. This was an act of grace! There was no consideration of the merit of the people thus chosen. There was, however, a stipulation of an obligation imposed on those chosen: "if you will obey me faithfully and keep My covenant" (19:5a JPS). Election brought responsibility! That is why we cannot think in terms of chapter 19 of Exodus calling the Hebrews into a covenantal relationship with God without including chapter 20 along with it. It is in the twentieth chapter that the Hebrews are given the moral code by which they must live, if they are to retain this covenant bond. This is what makes the Jews not simply a chosen people, but equally important, a choosing people. They accepted the heavy burden of the moral law when, at the foot of Sinai, they pronounced the words: "we will willingly do it" (Deuteronomy 5:24b JPS).

Why did the Hebrews accept this covenant relationship with God? According to the folklore found in Midrash Rabba to Exodus, many larger, more powerful nations were first offered these Ten Commandments as a covenant bond with God. The Rabbis tell us that one powerful nation read the commandments and declined to accept them because they were unwilling to put aside their other gods. Another nation rejected the commandments because they had become a mighty empire by conquering other nations and killing their leaders. Each nation approached by God had a different reason for declining to promise to live by God's moral law. Finally, almost in despair, God saw this wandering band of nomads and offered the Ten Command-ments to them, and the Hebrews accepted. But why? Was it, perhaps, because of a sense of loyalty to this God, Who had been in covenant relationship with their forefathers, the patriarchs? This is certainly a possibility. Or was it that this covenant brought with it not only responsibilities, but also opportunities? One of the most important opportunities was to occupy the land that this God controlled.

Rewards of Covenant Relationship

This idea of a god controlling specific areas of land was found not only in Hebrew tradition. Most of the gods of tribes and nations were thought to control certain territory. One of the grave problems that the Hebrews confronted if they worshiped only Yahweh was their fear of reprisals for ignoring the gods who had previously controlled the area they now occupied. Yet placating other gods, in order to assure themselves of bountiful crops, was a violation of their covenant with Yahweh. How to resolve this dilemma was one of the major burdens of the pre-exilic prophets.

The other benefit that acceptance of the covenant brought, the Hebrew sages taught, was that Yahweh led them into battle, riding on a throne on the ark of the covenant, to protect them as they sought to defend the land that God had given them. It is important to point out here that prospering of the crops and protection in war were not part of the covenantal bond, but rather resulted from it.

The promised land, however, was thought by the Hebrews to be an integral part of God's eternal covenant. The land was pledged to them by God as an everlasting possession (Genesis 13:15; 15:18; 17:7-8). And Hebrew Scriptures regard this promised land as a territory with specific geographic boundaries (Numbers 34:2-12; Ezekiel 47:13-20). Repeatedly Hebrew Scriptures stress that Yahweh is the true owner of the land and that the Hebrews possessed or inherited only that which rightfully belonged to their God. The continued possession of that land was always contingent on the Hebrew people obeying the moral law. When the people rebelled or disobeyed God's law and so were exiled, this never was interpreted as annulling the covenant. The prophets continually held out the promise of return when the people repented and renewed their covenant with Yahweh.

The Four Pillars of Covenant

Marvin Wilson, in *Our Father Abraham,* points out that "the concept of covenant within Judaism rests upon four foundational pillars: God, Torah, people, and land. Each interacts with and depends on the other. Far from the popular notion that Israel's covenant embraced only a spiritual dimension, it was in actuality 'tied to earth, life, land'" (p. 259).

Though the land was the symbol of the covenant bond between God and the Hebrews from the days of the patriarchs, Torah became an equally important symbol of the covenant when, according to tradition, Moses received it from God at Sinai. From that moment to the present, Jews have believed that God chose them to receive this Law, to live by it, and to transmit it to future generations. This conviction is expressed succinctly in a blessing recited before Torah is read in the synagogue: "Blessed is the Lord, our God, Ruler of the universe, Who has chosen us from all people by giving us His Torah. Blessed is the Lord, the Giver of the Torah."

Paul M. van Buren summarized the meaning of Torah for the Jewish people when he wrote:

> Living by Torah is Israel's grateful response to the covenant of grace made with Israel at Sinai by its Redeemer and Creator. The covenant is of grace because it is a gift of God's free love and is accepted by Israel as such. Living by Torah is by no means the way into this covenant; it is rather Israel's response to the gift of the covenant. It is how Israel lives because of its election, and that election is God's free gift. (Vol. 2, p. 76)

The people Israel now became the focus of the covenantal relationship with God. For many of the prophets, and especially for Second Isaiah, Israel was elected not only to occupy the promised land and to live by Torah, but to be God's witnesses and servants: "My witnesses are *you*—declares the Lord—My servant, whom I have chosen. To the end that you may take thought, and believe in Me, and understand that I am He" (Isaiah 43:10a JPS). To be a witness meant to be an example of holiness. Holiness here means separation—not physical separation necessarily, but spiritual separation. The goal of separation was to establish a special relationship with Yahweh, based on acceptance of Torah as the foundation upon which Israel was to live. Separation from other people was achieved in the performance of God's commandments. This is crucial to the witness; this is what it means to be a covenant people. Isaiah put it best when he wrote:

> Thus said the Lord:
> In an hour of favor I answer you.
> And on a day of salvation I help you—
> I created you and appointed you a covenant people—
> Restoring the land,
> Allotting anew the desolate holdings,
> Saying to the prisoners, "Go free,"
> To those who are in darkness, "Show yourselves."
> They shall pasture along the roads,
> On every bare height shall be their pasture.
>
> (Isaiah 49:8-9 JPS)

This is the hope that fulfillment of covenant, witnessing to God's word, will clear the way for that messianic day of justice and righteousness for all humankind.

The New Covenant

Finally, Jeremiah adds a whole new dimension to the Jewish people's covenant relationship with God:

> See, a time is coming—declares the Lord—when I will make a new covenant with the House of Israel and the House of Judah. It will not be like the covenant I made with their fathers, when I took them by the hand to lead them out of the land of Egypt, a covenant which they broke, so that I rejected them—declares the Lord. But such is the covenant I will make with the House of Israel after these days—declares the Lord: I will put My Teaching into their inmost being and inscribe it upon their hearts. Then I will be their God, and they shall be My people. No longer will they need to teach one

175

another and say to one another, "Heed the LORD"; for all of them, from the least of them to the greatest, shall heed Me—declares the LORD.

> For I will forgive their iniquities.
> And remember their sins no more.
> (Jeremiah 31:31-34 JPS)

Here we see the development of the deep spiritual covenant, not only with the people of Israel and Judah, but with the individual as well. It is still a covenant based on the Law given at Sinai, but that Law will be in the hearts of men and women, motivating them to "know" God in an intimate relationship. The covenant is now personalized, and enables the individual Israelite to enter into what Martin Buber termed an "I-Thou" relationship that was the unique privilege of the chosen ones.

Jewish Mission in Biblical Times

It is this sense of having been chosen by God for a special relationship as well as for a special mission that has sustained the people Israel through the centuries. It has provided a purpose for existence and for enduring the trials and persecutions of the ages. Never was there the concept within Judaism that the special relationship came about because of special merit. Nor have Jews felt that we were chosen to be blessed above other peoples. Rather were we chosen for a mission that began with glorifying the name of God throughout the world, bringing God's presence, God's omnipotence, and God's omniscience to all the nations on the earth. The ultimate goal of the Jews' mission was acknowledgment by all humankind of the universality of the One God. This was summarized best by the prophet Isaiah when he proclaimed: "Turn to Me and gain success, All the ends of the earth! For I am God, and there is none else" (Isaiah 45:22 JPS). This is the same message that we read in the teachings of Jeremiah and Ezekiel and of most of the other post-exilic prophets.

As a consequence of the message of the prophets, some peoples did recognize and accept Yahweh as their God. In the book of Zechariah there is an important verse that foresees this development: "Thus said the Lord of Hosts: In those days, ten men [meaning a multitude] from nations of every tongue will take hold—they will take hold of every Jew by a corner of his cloak and say, 'Let us go with you, for we have heard that God is with you'" (Zechariah 8:23 JPS). We do not know whether this verse indicates that at that point in history Jews were active in seeking to convert the pagan world to Judaism, or whether it was rather a matter of the pagans finding Yahweh as their God. In either case, this was a part of the utopian aspiration that we see in the words of the prophets Haggai and Zechariah, who were intent on bringing all nations to worship Yahweh at the second Temple in Jerusalem.

This mission goes in two entirely different directions after the return of many of the Jews from Babylon under the leadership of Ezra and Nehemiah. These men interpreted their mission in particularistic terms. They felt that it was essential to purify the Judean nation by removing the foreigners who had moved into Judea and had intermarried with those Jews who had remained in the land. Ezra and Nehemiah were intent on returning Samaritan wives and children to their own land, thus unifying the Judeans in reaffirming their special covenant relationship with Yahweh. Their mission was also to restore the Temple and there, for the first time, to teach Torah to the people on Mondays and Thursdays, when the farmers brought their wares to Jerusalem, and on the Sabbath. Ezra hoped that in hearing and living according to the words of Torah, the Jews might once again become a light unto the nations.

There were, however, those who disagreed violently with the philosophy of Ezra and Nehemiah. They conceived of the mission of the Jews in far more universalistic terms. The author of the book of Jonah was the first who conceived of Jews as being called to become messengers of God's word to the peoples of the world. This story of Jonah—seeking first to flee from the responsibility that God had placed on him, and ultimately, through God's providence, finding himself in the midst of the people whom God wanted to save from their sinfulness—is a striking example of the way in which Jews were to be instruments of God in bringing God's salvation to all of God's children.

The book of Ruth is most interesting in another way. The author concludes his book by stating that Obed, the son of Ruth,

177

the Moabite who became a Jew, would be the father of Jesse, the father of David. In Jewish tradition the Messiah would come someday from the house of David, a belief that is reiterated in the New Testament Gospels, which trace the lineage of Jesus back to David. The purpose of the author of Ruth seems clear in wanting to affirm that converts to Judaism had an important role in the realization of the ultimate goals of the Jewish people. There is a universalism in this messianic genealogy, just as there is universalism in Jonah's message that God seeks the repentance of all people in their accepting God's moral Law.

Jewish Mission in the Rabbinic Period

Continuing through the Jewish historical development, we find that mission as understood by the Pharisees in the rabbinic period becomes an important focus in their teachings. The Pharisees were particularistic in their mission in the sense that they were primarily concerned with bringing about a change in mind and heart that would enable the Judeans to enter the messianic age. At the same time we see in Matthew 23:15 that the Pharisees were proselytizers whose mission was "to traverse sea and land to make a single proselyte." The eventual hope of the Pharisees was to convert the entire Roman empire to Judaism. Though it appears that this hope was thwarted very quickly, we should realize that at one point in time approximately 20 percent of the population of the Roman empire was Jewish, and Jewish missionaries were zealous in seeking to convert the entire populace. Ultimately it was Christianity that succeeded in converting the Roman empire from its paganism to the worship of the One God. This competition between Jews and Christians in the missionary field was certainly one of the areas of sharp conflict between the two faiths.

As it became obvious by the first Nicean Council, and already in the early fourth century of the common era, when Constantine proclaimed Christianity a recognized religion of the Roman empire, that Judaism would not become the religion of the empire, the missionary focus of the Jews changed. The mission was to take both the written and the oral Torah to all peoples as the source of God's word which would guide them to pursue

God's paths of justice and compassion. This mission is expressed most beautifully in one of the oldest prayers in Jewish liturgy, found in our prayer books even to this day:

> May the time not be distant, O God, when Your name shall be worshipped in all the earth, when unbelief shall disappear and error be no more. Fervently we pray that the day may come when all shall turn to You in love, when corruption and evil shall give way to integrity and goodness, when superstition shall no longer enslave the mind, nor idolatry blind the eye, when all who dwell on earth shall know that You alone are God. O may all, created in Your image, become one in spirit and one in friendship, for ever united in Your service. Then shall Your kingdom be established on earth, and the word of Your prophet fulfilled: "The Lord will reign for ever and ever."

And the congregation responds:

> On that day the Lord shall be One and His name shall be One. (*Gates of Prayer,* p. 617)

Israel's Mission as Witness

Israel's mission, though, is not only as teachers of Torah but as witnesses to its teachings. There is a striking illustration of the concept of Israel's witness to the One God in a rabbinic interpretation of verse 4 of the sixth chapter of Deuteronomy. This verse contains the one absolute dogma in Jewish theology: God is, and God is One. The first word in that sentence in Hebrew is "Sh'ma," which means "hear." The Hebrew word consists of three letters, the last of which is the "ayin," and it is enlarged in all Torah scrolls. At the end of that sentence is the Hebrew word "echad," which means "one"; the last letter in that word is the "daled," and it is also enlarged in the Torah scroll. Put these two letters together and they form the word "ayd" in Hebrew, which means "witness." The Rabbis maintain that these two letters were enlarged by the Masoretes to emphasize that the mission of the Jews is to witness to this truth: there is One God for all humankind!

The witness does not end there, however. Equally important to the prophets is that the witness is to God's moral Law by which

God's children shall live and bring freedom and peace to all peoples. Isaiah proclaims this additional mission of the Jews when he writes:

> I the LORD, in My grace, have summoned you,
> And I have grasped you by the hand.
> I created you, and appointed you
> A covenant-people, a light of nations—
> Opening eyes deprived of light,
> Rescuing prisoners from confinement,
> From the dungeon those who sit in darkness.
> (Isaiah 42:6-7 JPS)

Jews have always considered our witness to the universal sovereignty of One God and to the supremacy of God's Law as enabling us to be God's co-workers in the establishment of God's kingdom on earth. We have not, however, been missionaries from the early fourth century C.E. to the latter half of the twentieth century. In recent times both Reform and Conservative Judaism have established educational centers in major metropolitan areas of the United States to encourage interested non-Jews to study Judaism with the possibility of their seeking conversion. Reform Judaism has also launched a national program of outreach to encourage non-Jewish spouses of Jews and other interested individuals to become active participants in Jewish congregational life. We welcome Jews by choice into our midst, though we do not pursue an aggressive missionary program such as that found in many Christian denominations.

Christian Mission from a Jewish Perspective

Jews recognize that Christians also have a strong sense of mission, primarily to enable non-Christians to find salvation through their acceptance of Jesus Christ as their personal Redeemer. We respect that mission, even though throughout the centuries Jews have been victims of overzealous proselytizers. In the Middle Ages especially, Jews were burned on fiery platforms for refusal to convert to Christianity. Over and over again, Jews were expelled from Christian countries because of their refusal to convert.

Fortunately, in recent times, Christian missionaries have been less ruthless in seeking to convert Jews. It must be said, however, in all candor, that Jews are still resentful of some Protestant denominations that sponsor aggressive programs for the conversion of Jews. Even more disturbing are the sects like "Jews for Jesus" who deceptively proselytize Jews, especially on college campuses, incorrectly stating that one can remain a Jew and still accept Jesus as the Christ. Jews believe that our covenant with God is an eternal covenant, that we have not been replaced by Christians who proclaim a new covenant, and that our mission remains as valid as it was when we received our Torah at Sinai.

Nevertheless we recognize that witness is a vital aspect of the mission of Christians and Jews. Let me heartily recommend to you the excellent volume *Christian Mission—Jewish Mission*, edited by Martin A. Cohen and Helga Croner. The essays were written by respected Jewish and Christian scholars, and they cover the wide spectrum of mission and missiology fairly and objectively. In his essay, "Contemporary Jewish Attitudes to Mission and Conversion," Rabbi Daniel F. Polish explains the important difference between active and passive witness. He suggests that active witness is manifest in activities undertaken to win someone over to one's own faith. On the other hand, passive witness is inner-directed. Polish says that "passive witness in its highest sense is those things which I do *l'shem shmayim*—for the sake of heaven." In other words, one may be as effective by exemplifying a Jewish or a Christian way of life, committed to our respective covenants with God, as by aggressively pursuing those who may be intimidated by anti-Semitic activities or by threats of eternal damnation.

We still live in a world unredeemed. Ours is a world in which hunger and homelessness are rampant in every corner of the earth. We are threatened with annihilation through pollution of our environment or from nuclear holocaust. There is still racial injustice and inequitable distribution of the natural resources of this good earth. In such a world Jews and Christians cannot relinquish the challenge of our respective missions. We can, however, pursue these missions with mutual respect and with an openness to all persons who wish to join us in our covenantal relationship with God.

UNDERSTANDING ELECTION, COVENANT, AND MISSION

A Christian Outlook

Few biblical notions have been as troubling to Jewish-Christian relations as those we are addressing in this chapter. In the course of the development of anti-Semitism throughout the Western world, one charge against the Jewish people used to justify this anti-Semitism has been that the Jews are a "clannish" people, that they stick together, that they hold themselves aloof from the societies in which they reside and earn their livings, and that they think themselves better than all other people. Groups in the "Christian" West, therefore, have banded together to exclude the Jews, claiming that such exclusion is warranted by Jewish aloofness and clannishness, which bring economic advantage to the Jews.

Christians often have forgotten that it is precisely their own exclusion of Jews that has required Jews to develop ways to counter the misunderstanding and mistreatment they have met. Christians too have perhaps been insufficiently attentive to what election and covenant have actually meant for them, according to the Scriptures. For this reason we wish to concentrate on election, covenant, and mission in Jewish and in Christian tradition.

Religious anti-Semitism—what Rabbi Falk called anti-Judaism above—also has some of its supposed justification in the idea of the election of the Jews by God as a special people in the world, and in the idea of a special pact or covenant between God and this one people. Not only has the Christian community often claimed to be the successor covenant people, elected by God to take the place of Israel because of the people's faithlessness. It often has rejected the very idea of divine election of a single people and covenant with this one people, in favor of God's universal covenant with all peoples. In this way it has been almost inevitable that Judaism would be looked upon as a narrow religion, claiming special privilege and favor for itself, not at all the religion of open invitation to all the world to join up, the religion of universal love, that Christianity has claimed to be.

Actually, a proper understanding of Jewish notions of election, covenant, and mission will indeed reveal differences between Jews and Christians on some aspects of these ideas. But the differences revealed give *no support at all* to anti-Semitism or anti-Judaism.

Israel's Election, Covenant, and Mission

Origin

Where did the idea arise that God had called Abraham from Mesopotamia and had promised him prosperity and many descendants and a particular land in which to dwell? Historical study cannot give an answer to this question. The ancestors of the Israelites probably were a people on the move in the Fertile Crescent, living among the settled peoples of this vast area, worshiping a deity whom they understood to be leading them to a destination not as yet certain and dealing with them intimately as the head of their extended family. References to the "God of the ancestors" dot the early statements about God in the stories of Abraham and Isaac and Jacob. This much may provide a background.

But that is a far cry from the notion that appears in Genesis 12:1-3, where Abraham is summoned by God to leave home and community supports and go into a land the very name and location of which he does not know. Abraham is told that God will grant prosperity and many descendants, but he is also told that he is to "*be* a blessing" (Genesis 12:2 RSV; emphasis added), not just to receive blessing. Election implies a purpose, a mission, that God has in the election. And, most important, Abraham is told that through him "all the families of earth" are to receive blessing.

Two features of God's choice or election of Abraham stand out.

183

First, Abraham is promised much, but much is demanded of him. He is to leave his community and land and to place his life in God's care. Election is free, but it carries consequences. And second, Abraham is to *be* a blessing wherever he goes, one through whom blessing is intended to flow out to all the families of humankind. This means that Abraham's election by God and God's covenant with him—the covenant of circumcision and of the land, as we noted above—entail accountability and responsibility. Abraham has to *be* what he is called to be, and he has to *be available* as a means of blessing and divine grace to others.

Exodus and Sinai

We have pointed out above that God's gift of the Torah is a gift of love and grace. Grace precedes law. The same applies to election and covenant. God sees Israel's oppression in Egypt and, out of love and a commitment to human freedom, frees the slaves. Deliverance from bondage is free, but it too has consequences. At Mount Sinai, one remarkable speech of God to Moses (Exodus 19:3-6) provides a marvelous combining of divine gift and love, on the one hand, and human obligation and commitment, on the other. God reminds Moses that Moses has seen what God did to the Egyptians (the whole struggle between God and the Pharaoh is summed up in this way!), and has also seen how God bore the people as if on the wings of an eagle, across the desert to the sacred mountain, bringing them *to God.* This reference of God's bringing the people "to Me" is a remarkable indication of the intimacy between God and people that election and covenant entail. God's tender care for the beloved people is unmistakable, and God's desire to share life with them is also clear. God wants the people bound to the divine Self in covenant, not just in order that they serve God, but because God loves them (a point made explicit in the language of Deuteronomy 7).

But then, just as in the case of Abraham, the commitment is laid down: "If you will listen to me and obey my voice, you shall be a special treasure to me—though all the earth is mine; you shall be to me a kingdom of priests and a holy nation." Israel *is* a special treasure to God, but Israel shall *all the more* be such a treasure as

Israel keeps faith with God, obeys the divine voice, holds fast to God's demands. This is an expansion of Israel's mission: for Israel is now clearly beloved by God, is God's special treasure, is cared for in a distinctive way, even though it is the case that all the earth—all the nations—belong to God. God is Israel's God, but the God who is Israel's God is also God of all.

The Prophets on Election, Covenant, and Mission

Throughout the entire corpus of Hebrew Scripture, including the interpretive work of Israel's prophets in particular, this view of election, covenant, and mission prevails. When the prophet Amos in the eighth century B.C.E. denounced the people of Israel for their sins, the people probably reminded him that they were, after all, God's people, bound to God in covenant. Surely God would not forget to be merciful to them, even though they had sinned. Amos' reply (3:2) is directly in accord with what we have seen from Genesis and Exodus. "You alone have I known from among all the families of the earth; therefore, I will punish you for all your iniquities." It is *because* they are God's people, God's elect, with whom God made covenant, that God must now hold them to account for their misdeeds. Israel's mission is to *be* Israel, recognizably so in the earth. Unfaithfulness to God and to the covenant is no way to be recognized as God's distinct people in the world! Election is free, but election has consequences.

The other side of this bond of love that carries such heavy demands, however, is that God too feels equally bound to Israel in love, according to Hebrew Scripture. Hosea 11:8-9 is one of the most passionate declarations of a love for sinful Israel that is so strong that it overrides divine wrath, or at least gives an entirely different character to God's exercise of divine judgment. "How can I give you up? . . . I am God, not a mortal . . . and I will not come as Destroyer!" Ezekiel too can speak of Jerusalem/Israel as having begun as a foundling child, cast alongside the road and utterly abandoned. God came by, did the duties of a midwife, provided for the child, and, as the child grew up, took her in marriage and wrapped the divine cloak around her (Ezekiel 16). Such love too has consequences, both in terms of judgment (Ezekiel is not loath to pronounce judgment) and in terms of

185

continuing love and mercy. Jeremiah speaks in similar terms (Jeremiah 2–3; 30–31). Similarly, Second Isaiah (Isaiah 40:1-11) opens with a declaration of God's pardon that takes account of Israel's having been punished *double* for all the people's sins. God addresses the heavenly host, calling on them to bring consolation to exiled Israel. The election of Israel assures that God, who loves Israel, holds this people in the divine care and will not forever leave them desolate. And Second Isaiah, more explicitly than any other prophet, speaks about Israel's mission to be a "light to the nations" (Isaiah 42:6; 49:6), one through whose suffering and humiliation the foreign nations are caused to come to their senses and make their confession of guilt before God (Isaiah 52:13–53:12).

Election and Covenant in the New Testament

Jesus on Election, Covenant, and Mission

Jesus' message is addressed to God's covenant people, the people elected by God. Jesus sees the promise of God approaching consummation even as he speaks and teaches and heals; and this promise has to do with Israel and, through Israel, with all the families of the earth. It is clear, then, that Jesus' message is a message addressed to his Jewish contemporaries, announcing that what God promised to the ancestors of old has now come to fruition. In the Gospel portrayals of Jesus there is no challenge to the notion of Israel's election by God and God's covenant with Israel. There are, as in the case of Israel's prophets, reminders of the demands that election and covenant bring. Israel must *be* the people of God that God has called them to be. As the message of Jesus takes root among his disciples, this message is recognized to be a message of universal import, one that must be borne to the ends of the earth. The early Christian community understands this mission to spread the Good News to the ends of the earth to have been given to it by the risen Christ (see Matthew 28:16-20; Acts 1:6-8). The divine Spirit impels the community outward from Jerusalem to the ends of the earth, for the Good News of God's love is recognized to belong to all peoples everywhere.

186

First Peter

First Peter has a detailed interpretation of Exodus 19:3-6, giving the passage an interpretation for the gentile world that conforms well to its meaning for the Jewish people, although the context can suggest that the Christian community is now the *replacement* of the community of Israel. This letter to churches in northern Asia Minor stresses the need for the Christian community to live in the midst of a pagan environment as those set apart by God's election, brought out of darkness into God's "marvelous light" (I Peter 2:9). Once they were no people at all, but now they are God's people; once they had not known divine mercy, but now they do. One can see here how this Christian evangelist uses Israel's election by God to provide a fundamental characterization of the Christian community in a Hellenistic environment. The Christian community, like the Jewish, must be recognizably what it has been made to be by God's action. Chosen by God out of sheer divine love and grace ("once you were no people"), this community is now "a chosen race, a royal priesthood, a holy nation, a people of God's own possession."

The Christian impetus clearly shows up in the mandate stated in First Peter: "that you may declare the wonderful deeds of the One who called you out of darkness into God's marvelous light." The Christian community is to *be*, clearly and publicly, what God has created it to be. It is also to declare the glory of this deed of God for all to hear and know. Christianity has this impetus to speak about God's glories before the world, even as it embodies these glories in the way it lives its life.

Paul on Election, Covenant, and Mission

Paul is the New Testament writer who most deeply struggles with the question of how Israel's mission and that of the Christian church differ. From his point of view, Israel and the Christian community are both elect, and both partake of a covenant with God. The church's election derives from that of Israel, but not in the sense that it takes the place of Israel's election. God's covenant with Israel, though broken and rejected from the human side, remains unbroken and irrevocable from God's side (Romans 11:29).

It is not entirely clear how Paul distinguished the mission of

Israel and that of the church. He himself is clearly drawn into the Christian community *as a Jew,* and he does not reject his identity as a Jew. But he is equally clearly not committed to a mission among the Jewish communities of the Mediterranean world to cause all Jews to become Christians. His is a mission to the gentile world. His initial presentations of the gospel do regularly begin in the synagogues of Asia Minor and Europe, but the invitation that rings out is addressed to the gentiles, the non-Jewish members of the communities. His letters show some conflict with Peter and others who would require these gentile converts to take up Jewish customs and observances. The book of Acts describes a kind of resolution of the conflict, by which some minimal observances are adopted by the new converts, at least for a time (Acts 15:6-29). But clearly Paul insists on a very great degree of freedom in the lives of the gentile converts to Christian faith (see I Corinthians 9, for example). The mission of the Christian community is to convert pagans not to Judaism but to Christianity. Jews are invited to become a part of the Christian community, but the mission of the church to Judaism is of a different sort than that to the gentile world.

A Christian "Mission to the Jews"?

Paul's dealings with the Jewish community, as recorded in the New Testament, offer guidelines for the only appropriate Christian "mission to the Jews." Paul engaged in intensive debate and conversation with the Jewish leaders of his day, seeking to see how the Christian revelation related to the promise of God to Israel, to the Torah, to religious rites, and to the nature of Christian freedom. His letters, and especially the great Letter to the Romans, show the depth of this effort of Paul to understand how he, a Jew, could and must remain a Jew while also being elected by God to be one of the apostles of Jesus Christ, the apostle to the gentiles. No doubt, changes in his understanding occurred over time. The language of Galatians is different from that of Romans on a number of these points. On the whole it may be said that Paul affirmed the necessity for the Jewish community and the Christian community to continue the struggle over the meaning of the new life that God was extending to the world in

Christ. Israel remained Israel and remained the Israel of God, a people who could count upon the promises of God. Israel was in God's care, and Israel's destiny was fixed in the divine purpose. But the new life extended in Jesus Christ also included the gentile world, since, from one point of view (the need for God's saving acts), Jew and gentile were entirely the same in God's sight (Romans 10:12).

Paul's most profound dealings with Christian election, covenant, and mission have to do with the mystery of divine love and acceptance known by the Christian community in association with sharing life with Christ (see especially II Corinthians 5:14-21). To be "in Christ" is to be a new creation, to partake in a world made new. This mystic depth-meaning of life in Christ was something that Paul wanted all persons to experience. To this extent he was eager for conversation with Jews as well as with gentiles, for he believed that he had a message and an experience to share that would be of value to any person, to any community.

But even here it is important to recognize that Paul would be astonished to see anything like Christian "missions to the Jews" such as those launched in the nineteenth century and continued in some Christian circles to this day. For those "missions" set out to deny the truth and power and legitimacy of the Jewish community's faith and religious understandings and practices. Surely that is a position that the "apostle to the gentiles" would reject out of hand. It should also be rejected by Christians today.

Election, Covenant, and Mission in a Pluralistic World

What are we to say about the "uniqueness" of Judaism and Christianity today? The issue is more readily addressed by the Jewish community, since the practice through the centuries has been to be a "light before the nations" rather than a "light that the nations should accept as theirs." Christian missionary activity has tended for too long (though the situation has radically changed during the last fifty or so years) to be of the latter sort. The adherents of other religions or the non-religious are invited by some forms of Christian missionary activity to abandon their present religion and accept the religion of those who witness to

189

them, or to abandon their non-religious position in favor of the religion of the witness.

It is understandable that those whose lives have been transformed by confrontation with the holy God should want to share with others the power and the truth of that confrontation. How can they *not* speak of a truth and a power and a presence that has been the very salvation of their existence? But there are two aspects of the sharing of such essentially true and ultimate disclosures that need to be kept in mind. The first is that such experiences belong to the religious traditions of the entire human community. We cannot insist that ours, which certainly claims us ultimately, is an experience that can only come through the traditions and scriptures and experiences of our community. As a Christian, I believe in the depth-truth of the revelation of God in Jesus Christ. But I am unable to say to the adherents of other religions, or to the non-religious, "My depth-truth is also yours."

The second thing to be said, which follows from the first perhaps, is that our own depth-truths may come to us as ultimate, but they also come to us as grounded in depth-Mystery that remains Mystery even as revelation takes place. Our *expressions* of the truth, power, and import of the disclosure are not adequate to convey the full dimensions of the disclosure. What is revealed is Mystery, and it remains Mystery even after the revelation takes place and claims us.

Jews and Christians, then, share a common understanding of election and covenant, and their understandings of God's mission for them in the world are also similar. But the Christian community, charged as it is to take the Good News to the whole world, has to be a "light before the nations" and also a "light to the nations," in the sense that it must seek every opportunity to share this depth-Mystery with all who will lend an ear. As it does so, it needs clearly to bear in mind that sharing this depth-Mystery with the Jewish community differs from all other sharing. The Jewish and the Christian communities engage in *dialogue about a Mystery that each knows and shares.* Differences are profound and must be acknowledged and explored.

One last reminder may be in order. As Christians and Jews learn more about the religious existence of other peoples and groups, they may both discover that there is an analogous kinship between the Jewish and Christian understandings and those of all other potential partners in dialogue and debate. Should that happen, then it would be evident that all religious communities stand equally near to and distant from the center of the depth-Mystery. There are many today who believe that this is so.

Suggested Readings

Cohen, M., and H. Croner. *Christian Mission—Jewish Mission.*
Klenicki, L., and G. Wigoder. *A Dictionary of the Jewish-Christian Dialogue.*
Küng, H., and W. Kasper. *Christians and Jews.*
Oesterreicher, J. *Brothers in Hope,* vol. 5.
Pawlikowski, J. *Christ in the Light of the Christian-Jewish Dialogue,* chapter 7.
Talmage, F. *Disputation and Dialogue.*
Tanenbaum, M. *Evangelicals and Jews in Conversation.*
Van Buren, P. A Theology of the Jewish-Christian Reality: Part II—*A Christian Theology of the People Israel.*

CHAPTER NINE

CONCLUSION

Two colleagues and friends, one Jewish and one Christian, have sought to show that much is to be gained from exchanges between Jews and Christians, if they are ready to state the views of their respective traditions as clearly as they can and if they are ready to give serious attention to the partner's views. We have chosen to put ourselves in the place of the other and state what we understand, not only about our own tradition, but also about the partner's tradition.

We recognize that some will take exception to our ways of presenting one or both of the traditions. We have not attempted to give a "consensus" version of Judaism and Christianity. Rather, we have here done our best to speak out of our respective traditions, giving not just our opinions but a critical reading of the tradition that we believe is faithful to its central affirmations. We may have been too irenic, too eager to see the best in the other's tradition, and too ready to downplay points of difference. But we hope that, on the whole, we have been faithful to our intention: to show that Jews and Christians have much to gain by Jewish/Christian dialogue.

There are many Jews and Christians, however, who do not believe that such dialogue accomplishes much. Some, in fact, choose not to engage in such efforts. One of the queries often put to discussants in Jewish/Christian relations is whether the discussions are not too often laid out on the grounds of Christian theological concerns. Are Jews really interested in questions of Christian theology, especially such questions as the Trinity, theories of Christian atonement, redemption from sin, and the like? And even if they are, are these kinds of questions the ones that have troubled and bedeviled the relations of Jews and

193

Christians through the centuries? Moreover, is the record of Christian anti-Semitism not so long and so pervasive that recent efforts are unlikely to change anything fundamentally? And most urgently, has not the Holocaust so changed the world situation that Christians have no right to expect to be able to carry on discussions and debates with Jews in the normal terms and tones of civilized discussion?

Questions and objections of this sort must not be ignored. The two authors have indeed been challenged by persons with views of this sort in the course of their public presentations, and they have done their best to take such comments and concerns seriously in their replies.

Are We Addressing the Right Concerns?

We can deal briefly with the first kind of concern—whether the questions and issues being raised are couched in Christian terms that are of little real interest or value to Jews. Certainly, the history of the relations of Jews and Christians is a story from which all should be able to learn, following the dictum that those who do not learn from history are doomed to repeat it. The story is, on the whole, a grim account of misrepresentation and mistreatment of the Jewish people by the Christian community. It would be good to have scholars work on this story with an eye to identifying more of the friends of the Jews who must surely have been active in Christian communities through the centuries. As in the case of the Holocaust, so in general: there were Christians and other non-Jews who showed humanity to the Jews and did not follow the widespread pattern of misrepresentation and mistreatment. But there were entirely too few intellectual and spiritual leaders in times past who were dealing positively with the continuing place of the Jewish people in lands where Christianity was the dominant or the established religion. Islamic lands seem to have a somewhat better record in their treatment of Jewish subjects, though the record is mixed indeed within the Islamic world.

Every generation of Christians needs to review this painful story, including its most unbearable part, the story of the Holocaust, in order to find the impulse and the strength to say to living Jews today, "I am sorry." Church bodies and church officials need to find ways to do the same through their own public statements, through liturgies and confessions, and in their specific statements concerning the relations of Judaism and Christianity. One excellent way that is becoming more and more widespread within the Christian community is to observe the Days of Remembrance of the Holocaust, the Shoah, now a recognized holiday in many parts of the world. It is noteworthy that the U.S. government was ahead of most of the churches in giving lasting remembrance of the Holocaust through the appointment of the Holocaust Memorial Council and the building of the Holocaust Museum in Washington (to open in 1993). This museum honors and memorializes all of those who were put to death in accordance with the "Master Race" ideology of National Socialism. It also keeps in remembrance the survivors, the betrayers, the rescuers, and the liberators. A comparable memorial erected by the worldwide Christian community has not yet been announced.

What of our other topics? Few would question the value of our examining our scriptures, notions of covenant and election, the State of Israel, and the Holocaust. Those issues loom large in the actual conflicts and controversies that go on today, within the Christian and the Jewish communities and between the two communities. And as we noted above (chapters 5 and 6) there is a larger interest today on the part of members of the Jewish community in how to address strictly theological questions. This interest arises in part from the unmistakable importance of religious fundamentalism and its part in political and social developments in Israel.

Local communities should of course be encouraged to select their own particular areas of special concern. In doing so, it is important for both parties to be explicit about these areas of concentration, so that neither the Christian nor the Jewish agenda dominates the discussion.

Is There Really Any Point in Jewish/Christian Conversations?

The other question is more sobering and formidable. It often takes two different forms. There are those who say that, this side of the Holocaust, formal or even informal organized discussions of faith between Jews and Christians can get nowhere. The Holocaust is an event of such magnitude that both communities have to address in the most searching ways possible what faith in God can mean this side of the Holocaust. Some Jewish writers say that within the Jewish community such searching addressing of the question of God, of religious faith as such, is going on, but they see little sign of its going on within Christianity.

Not enough is being done within the Christian community, but much is. One needs only to review the bibliography at the end of the book in order to see how much fresh effort is under way. The most comprehensive is a three-volume work by Paul van Buren, who is completing an entire "theology of the Jewish-Christian reality" (a fourth and concluding volume is in preparation). There the Holocaust receives direct address in connection with Christology and other Christian doctrines. Studies of the Hebrew Scriptures by Christian scholars are also seeking afresh to address the question of God's silence in the face of evil, an issue powerfully laid out in Scripture. In addition, efforts to frame a theology that gives larger place to religious and cultural pluralism are proving valuable in addressing the world-shattering event of the Holocaust.

Other Jewish voices say that they take heart from some Christian developments (the encyclical *Nostra aetate*, for example) only to have their hopes shattered by others (the convent at Auschwitz, for example, or the Vatican's refusal to recognize the State of Israel). May it not be true, they cannot help wondering, that on the whole the Christian community is irreformably unsympathetic to Judaism, unwilling if not in fact unable *not* to be anti-Semitic?

In light of such concerns, which are real and weighty, what can one recommend? The two of us maintain that persons who believe that nothing of great value can result from Jewish/Christian relations should still persevere, join in, and carry on with such discussions, such efforts to work together, such efforts to reduce prejudice and misunderstanding. They should not give up, because they may be wrong. The two of us believe that the two communities have much of positive value to learn from each other. Our association over thirty years has brought about fundamental changes in the ways in which we view *both* religious communities and understand and interpret their central affirmations. Those who hold that not much can be expected from Jewish/Christian relations have evidence on their side; we would not deny that for a moment. Over and again, gains seem to be offset by setbacks. But in our judgment there is progress. Virtually all of the Christian denominations now have, or are currently completing, statements on Judaism and the Jewish people that seek to correct longstanding misperceptions and misstatements. Studies of Scripture, church history, and theology in many North American theological schools are now carried on in such a way as to confront and challenge anti-Semitic statements and inferences.

But there can never be enough direct contact between Jews and Christians who engage to know one another better, discuss the issues of faith and life's meaning that most concern them, and attempt to see what may lie in their common religious heritage that would help them, together, to enrich their faith. Joint study of the Hebrew Scriptures, of the New Testament, and of Talmud and Midrash—difficult as it is, and demanding—will be immensely rewarding for those who will undertake it.

As Christians who have not been involved in Jewish/Christian exchanges take their first steps in this direction, they may soon be led to say to their Jewish colleagues: "I am sorry. I am sorry for the long history of Christian mistreatment and persecution of the Jewish people. I am sorry that German Christians, among many others, acquiesced in the Master Race theory of National Socialism and did not say, 'If these steps are to be taken against the Jewish people, then they have to be taken against me, for as a Christian I belong with them.' I am sorry that Christians all too frequently still look upon Judaism as a religion that no longer has any distinctive place in the world, now that Christianity has come. In short, I am sorry for what my Christian forebears and contemporaries have done to Jews. And I am sorry for my own part in all this."

By the same token, there are surely Jews who may wish to say to their Christian colleagues: "I, too, have been wrong. I have been so blinded by the hurts of anti-Semitism that I have failed to recognize the courageous defenders and the good friends that we have within the Christian community. I have allowed my fears and my suspicions so to affect my relationships with Christians that I have lost trust in their integrity. I have felt such deep hurt because of hatred and venom in attacks by those who presumed to speak and act in the name of Christ, that I have for too long blocked out any relationship to Jesus as teacher and prophet in our Jewish tradition."

The dialogue has to be engaged in on equal terms. Each community has a contribution to make to the other, and each partner should expect both to give and to receive. After thirty years of such dialogue with each other, the authors are confident that each understands better today not only the religion of the partner in dialogue but his own religion as well. As the dialogue illuminates one's central beliefs and affirmations, one discovers more and more commonalities; moving toward one another, in fact, means moving toward the central reality of the one God.

BIBLIOGRAPHY

Almog, Shmuel. *Antisemitism Through the Ages*. Oxford: Pergamon, 1988.
Baeck, Leo. *Judaism and Christianity*. Philadelphia: Jewish Publication Society, 1960.
Barth, Markus. *Israel and the Church*. Richmond, Va.: John Knox Press, 1969.
Boers, Hendrikus. *Who Was Jesus?* San Francisco: Harper, 1989.
Bokser, Ben Zion. *Judaism and the Christian Predicament*. New York: Alfred A. Knopf, 1967.
Borowitz, Eugene. *Contemporary Christologies: A Jewish Response*. New York: Paulist Press, 1980.
Bratton, Fred G. *The Crime of Christendom*. Boston: Beacon Press, 1969.
Buber, Martin. *Two Types of Faith*. New York: Macmillan, 1986.
———. *The Prophetic Faith*. New York: Harper, 1949.
Charlesworth, James. *Jesus Within Judaism*. New York: Doubleday, 1988.
Cohen, Martin, and Helga Croner, eds. *Christian Mission—Jewish Mission*. New York: Paulist Press, 1982.
Croner, Helga, ed. *Stepping Stones to Further Jewish-Christian Relations*. New York: Paulist Press, 1977.
———. *More Stepping Stones to Jewish-Christian Relations*. New York: Paulist Press, 1985.
DeCorneille, Roland. *Christians and Jews—The Tragic Past and the Hopeful Future*. New York: Harper & Row, 1966.
Eckardt, A. Roy. *Elder and Younger Brothers—The Encounter of Jews and Christians*. New York: Scribner's, 1967.
Erickson, Robert P. *Theologians Under Hitler*. New Haven: Yale University Press, 1985.
Falk, Harvey. *Jesus the Pharisee*. New York: Paulist Press, 1985.
Flannery, Edward H. *The Anguish of the Jews*. New York: Paulist Press, 1985.
Gager, John G. *The Origins of Anti-Semitism*. New York: Oxford, 1983.
Horsley, Richard A. *Jesus and the Spiral of Violence*. San Francisco: Harper, 1987.
———, and John S. Hanson. *Bandits, Prophets, and Messiahs: Popular Movements at the Time of Jesus*. San Francisco: Harper, 1985.
Isaac, Jules. *Jesus and Israel*. New York: Holt, Rinehart & Winston, 1971.
Jacobs, Walter. *Christianity Through Jewish Eyes*. Cincinnati: HUC Press, 1974.
Johnson, Paul. *A History of the Jews*. San Francisco: Harper, 1987.
Keck, Leander. *A Future for the Historical Jesus*. Nashville: Abingdon Press, 1971. (Books on Demand, University Microfilms International, Ann Arbor, MI.)
Klausner, Joseph. *Jesus of Nazareth*. Trans. Herbert Danby. New York: Menorah Publishing Co., 1978.

Bibliography

————. *From Jesus to Paul.* Trans. William Stinespring, New York: Menorah Publishing Co., 1978.

Klenicki, Leon, and Geoffrey Wigoder, eds. *A Dictionary of the Jewish-Christian Dialogue.* New York: Paulist Press, 1984.

Küng, Hans, and Walter Kasper, eds. *Christians and Jews.* New York: The Seabury Press, 1974.

Lapide, Pinchas. *Israelis, Jews and Jesus.* New York: Doubleday, 1979.

————. *The Resurrection of Jesus: A Jewish Perspective.* Minneapolis: Augsburg, 1983.

Lohse, Edward. *The New Testament Environment.* Nashville: Abingdon, 1976.

Lowenstein, Rudolph M. *Christians and Jews: A Psychoanalytic Study.* New York: International Universities Press, 1952.

Neusner, Jacob. *Judaism and Christianity in the Age of Constantine.* Chicago: University of Chicago Press, 1987.

————. *From Politics to Piety: The Emergence of Pharisaic Judaism.* Englewood Cliffs, N.J.: Prentice-Hall, 1973.

Odeberg, Hugo. *Pharisaism and Christianity.* St. Louis: Concordia Publishing House, 1943.

Oesterreicher, John M., ed. *Brothers in Hope.* The Bridge Judaeo-Christian Studies, vol. 5. New York: Herder & Herder, 1970.

Parkes, James. *The Conflict of the Church and the Synagogue.* New York: Macmillan, 1969.

————. *Foundations of Judaism and Christianity.* Chicago: Quadrangle Books, 1960.

————. *The Jew and His Neighbor: A Study of the Causes.* London: Student Christian Movement Press, 1938.

————. *Jews, Christians and the World Tomorrow.* Southhampton: Parkes Library, 1967.

Pawlikowski, John T. *Christ in the Light of the Christian-Jewish Dialogue.* New York: Paulist Press, 1982.

————. *What Are They Saying About Christian-Jewish Relations?* New York: Paulist Press, 1980.

Peck, Abraham J., ed. *Jews and Christians After the Holocaust.* Philadelphia: Fortress Press, 1982. (Books on Demand, University Microfilms International, Ann Arbor, MI.)

Petuchowski, Jakob, and Michael Brocke, eds. *The Lord's Prayer and Jewish Liturgy.* New York: Seabury, 1978.

Pfeffer, Leo. *Creeds in Competition.* New York: Harper, 1958; reprinted 1978 by Greenwood.

Plaut, W. Gunther, ed. *The Torah: A Modern Commentary.* New York: Union of American Hebrew Congregations, 1981.

Rivkin, Ellis. *A Hidden Revolution.* Nashville: Abingdon, 1978.

Rogow, Arnold A. *The Jew in a Gentile World.* New York: Macmillan, 1961.

Roth, Cecil. *A History of the Marranos.* Philadelphia: The Jewish Publication Society of America, 1932; reprint edition by Arno Press, New York, 1975.

Roth, J. K., and M. Berenbaum. *Holocaust: Religious and Philosophical Implications.* New York: Paragon House, 1989.

Rousseau, Richard W., ed. *Christianity and Judaism: The Deepening Dialogue.* Scranton, Pa.: Ridge Row Press, 1983.

Ruether, Rosemary R. *Faith and Fratricide—The Theological Roots of Anti-Semitism.* New York: Seabury, 1974.

Sandmel, Samuel. *When a Jew and Christian Marry.* Philadelphia: Fortress, 1977.

————. *Judaism and Christian Beginnings.* New York: Oxford University Press, 1978.

Bibliography

―――. *A Jewish Understanding of the New Testament*. Cincinnati: HUC Press, 1974.
―――. *Anti-Semitism in the New Testament?* Philadelphia: Fortress Press, 1978.
―――. *The Hebrew Scriptures*. New York: Oxford University Press, 1978.
Silver, A. H. *Where Judaism Differs*. Macmillan, 1989.
Simon, Marcel. *Verus Israel*. New York: Oxford University Press, 1986.
Steinsaltz, Adin. *The Essential Talmud*. New York: Basic Books, 1982.
Talmage, F. E., ed. *Disputation and Dialogue: Readings in the Jewish-Christian Encounter*. New York: Ktav, 1975.
Tanenbaum, Marc H., ed. *Evangelicals and Jews in Conversation*. New York: Harper, 1958.
Tcherikover, Victor. *Hellenistic Civilization and the Jews*. New York: Atheneum, 1970.
Thoma, Clemens. *A Christian Theology of Judaism*. New York: Paulist Press, 1980.
Van Buren, Paul M. *A Theology of the Jewish-Christian Reality, Part I: Discerning the Way*. New York: Seabury, 1980.
―――. *A Theology of the Jewish-Christian Reality, Part II: A Christian Theology of the People Israel*. New York: Seabury, 1983.
―――. *A Theology of the Jewish-Christian Reality, Part III: Christ in Context*. San Francisco: Harper, 1988.
Vermes, Geza. *Jesus and the World of Judaism*. Philadelphia: Fortress, 1983.
―――. *Jesus the Jew*. Minneapolis: Augsburg/Fortress, 1981.
Weiss-Rosmarin, Trude. *Jewish Expressions on Jesus*. New York: Ktav, 1977.
Williamson, Clark M. *Has God Rejected His People?* Nashville: Abingdon, 1982.
Wilson, Marvin. *Our Father Abraham*. Grand Rapids: Wm. B. Eerdmans Publishing Co., 1989.
Wyman, David. *The Abandonment of the Jews*. New York: Pantheon, 1984.
Yadin, Yigael. *The Temple Scroll*. New York: Random House, 1985.
Yaseen, Leonard C. *The Jesus Connection—To Triumph over Anti-Semitism*. New York: Crossroad, 1985.

INDEX

Aaron, 158
Abraham: call of, 21; as first Jew, 53; God's covenant with, 57, 82, 136, 146-47, 157, 170-71, 183-84
Acts, book of, 71-72
Adam, typological interpretation of, 68
Adler, Morris, 17
Ahasuerus, King, 127
Albright, William F., *History, Archaeology and Christian Humanism*, 132
Alexander the Great, 32, 61
Althaus, Paul, 133
Amos, the prophet, 22, 31, 57, 83, 185
Anti-Christian bias, stereotypes of, 15
Antiochus Epiphanes, 33, 61, 68
Anti-Semitism: stereotypes of, 14-15; first instance of, 127; in the Middle Ages, 35-37; religious, 129-30
Apocrypha, the, 60-61, 65, 72, 73, 74-75
Arabs: attitude of, toward Jews, 15; Christian sympathy for, 166-67; in World War I, 148; relations of, with State of Israel, 39, 131, 139, 145, 149-51, 154-55
Armenians, slaughter of, 138
Ashi, 35, 62-63
Assyrian conquest of Israel, 22, 160
Avenue of Righteousness (monument), 133

Babylonia, conquest of Judah, 22, 160
Babylonian Exile, 23, 31-32, 59
Balfour, Lord, 148
Bar Kokhba, 44, 108
Bel and the Dragon, 61
Blacks, American, and Jews, 15
Bonhoeffer, Dietrich, 133
Brueggemann, Walter, 156
Buber, Martin, *I and Thou*, 86, 176; *The Prophetic Faith*, 59-60

Calvin, John, 47
Camp David Accords, 150
Christian church school literature, 21-23, 26
Christianity and Judaism: The Deepening Dialogue (Rousseau), 155
Christianity: as successor to Israel, 21-32, 44-48, 135-36, 160-61, 182-83, 187-89; in the Holy Land, 29, 42-46; Jewish heritage of, 14, 41-43, 50; and proselytes, 16, 180-81

Christian Mission—Jewish Mission (Cohen and Croner, eds.), 181
Christian Theology of the People Israel (van Buren), 110
Christ-killers, Jews as. *See* Deicide, charges of; Crucifixion of Jesus
Christology, issue of, 18
Circumcision, 184
Conservative Jews, 64, 180
Constantine, Emperor, 35-36, 45-46, 129-30, 135, 178-79
Constitution, U.S., 49
Coughlin, Father, 38, 128
Counter-Reformation, 47-48
Covenant, the: between God and the Jews, 30, 50, 53, 56-58, 81-82, 94, 156, 169, 173-74; demands of, 21, 31, 147, 159-60, 172-75, 184-85, 186, 189-90; Four Pillars of, 174-75, universality of, 84, 171, 177, 182-83, 186
Creation story, 30, 80-81
Crucifixion of Jesus, 121, 128, 136. *See also* Deicide, charges of; Romans, responsibility of, for crucifixion
Crusades, the, 36, 130, 164
Cyrus the Persian, 22, 31

Daniel, book of, 61, 68, 71-72
David, King, 104, 177-78
Day of Consummation, 116, 117-18, 119, 163. *See also* New Age, the
Dead Sea Scrolls, 65, 75-76, 107-8, 115. *See also* Essenes; Qumran
Deicide, charges of, 14, 38, 136. *See also* Crucifixion of Jesus; Romans, responsibility of, for crucifixion
Denmark, 131
Deputy, The (Hochhuth), 131-32
Deuteronomy, book of, 56
Domitian, Emperor, 44
Dreyfus, Alfred, 147-48
Dutch West Indies Company, 37-38, 128

Ecclesiastes, book of, 60
Ecclesiasticus, book of, 61
Egypt, Hebrews in, 157-58
Elijah, the prophet, 22, 57
Elisha, the prophet, 57
England, 36-37, 47, 127, 148-49
Enlightenment, the, 48
Enuma Elish, 80-81

203

Index

Ericksen, Robert P., *Theologians Under Hitler*, 132
Esau, 21
Esdras, II book of, 61
Essenes: community of, 34, 41, 42, 44, 114-16; relationship with Jesus, 107-8, 116-18
Esther, book of, 127
Evangelical Christians, 145, 165
Ezekiel, book of, 73; the prophet, 58, 111, 185-86
Ezra, the prophet, 30, 31-32, 53, 56, 73, 177

Fackenheim, Emil, 141
Faith and Fratricide (Ruether), 17-18
Fathers, early church, 129
Ferdinand and Isabella, 130
Flood narrative, 30
Ford, Henry, 38, 128
France, 36-37, 47, 127, 147-48

Gates of Prayer, 79, 179
Gemara, the, 35, 62-63, 74-75
Germany, anti-Semitism in, 130-33, 136-37. *See also* Holocaust, the; Nazi Party, the; Hitler, Adolf
God: (Christian concepts of): as Incarnate, 93; as Savior, 93-94; as Trinity, 95-97; (Jewish concepts of): as Creator, 80-81; as One, 79, 83, 86-87, 95, 97, 179-80; as personal, 82-83, 85-86; as universal, 84-85
Golden-calf narrative, 30-31
Gospels, the, 70-71

Habakkuk Commentary, 67-68
Hadrian, Emperor, 44
Hagar, 146-47
Haman, 127
Hebrew Scriptures: as history, 53; canons of, 65, 72-73; Christian use of, 47, 54-55, 65-69, 73-74, 137; and oral tradition, 27. *See also* Old Testament
Hellenism, 32-34, 61, 111, 113-14
Herzl, Theodore, 148
Heschel, Abraham, *God in Search of Man*, 16
Hidden Revolution, A (Rivkin), 111
Hillel, Rabbi, 62, 103, 117
Hirsch, Emanuel, 132, 133
History, Archaeology and Christian Humanism (Albright), 132

Hitler, Adolf, 48, 130-33, 137. *See also* Holocaust, the; Nazi Party; Germany
Hochhuth, Rolf, *The Deputy*, 131-32
Holland, 131
Holocaust, the, 15, 39, 49-50, 138-40. *See also* Hitler, Adolf; Germany; Nazi Party
Hosea, the prophet, 31, 57
Huldah, the prophetess, 56
Hyrcanus, John, 32

I and Thou (Buber), 86
Ibn Ezra, Rabbi, 63-64
Isaac, 21, 146-47
Isaiah, book of, 22, 31, 55, 57, 58
Ishmael, 146-47
Israel: as God's people, 20 (*see also* Covenant); Northern Kingdom of, 22, 57, 58, 160; State of: Christian responses to, 15, 50, 140-41, 145, 151-53, 164-66; establishment of, 139, 146, 149-50; political goals of, 154-56. *See also* Arabs, relations of, with

Jerome, 73-74
Jerusalem, 23, 44
Jesus: as a Jew, 102, 178, 186; Christian relationship to, 113-24; Jewish relationship to, 25-26, 102-12, 129
Jewish Bible. *See* Hebrew Scriptures
Jewish revolts, 41, 43, 44
Job, book of, 60
John, Gospel of, 44, 70, 116, 120
John XXIII, 39
John the Baptist, 108, 115, 117
Jonah, book of, 32, 177
Joseph, 137, 157
Josephus, 107, 111, 113-14
Judah (Southern Kingdom), 57, 58

Kingship, establishment of, in Israel, 58-60
Kittel, Gerhard, 132-33
Kristallnacht, 131
Ku Klux Klan, 38

Law, the, 20-21, 35, 97-98. *See also* Covenant, the; Torah
League of Nations, 148-49
Levy, Asser, 128
Liberal Jews, 30, 150
Luke-Acts, 43-44

204

INDEX OF SCRIPTURE REFERENCES

Index

Christian Scriptures (New Testament)